Rebecca Greenstreet was called to the Bar in 2013 and is a personal injury and clinical negligence specialist. She is a member of Hardwicke chambers and lives in Sydney, Australia.

During her time in practice Rebecca acted for both claimants and defendants in clinical negligence matters and in all aspects of personal injury, including road traffic accidents, fraud, occupiers' liability, employers' liability, historic sexual abuse, industrial disease and inquests. She regularly appeared in costs matters arising in such claims, including both QOCS and fixed costs arguments.

Rebecca has a keen interest in medical ethics, previously volunteering for the Patient Advisory Liaison Service which provided a complaints resolution service within a busy and struggling hospital. She read Law at St Hugh's College Oxford before undertaking a Masters Degree in Health Care Ethics and Law at Manchester University. Rebecca's post-graduate dissertation provided inspiration for this book, exploring whether the law governing awards for child rearing costs in wrongful birth and wrongful conception claims was satisfactory.

A Practical Guide to Wrongful Conception, Wrongful Birth and Wrongful Life Claims

A Practical Guide to Wrongful Conception, Wrongful Birth and Wrongful Life Claims

Rebecca Greenstreet
BA Hons (Oxon), MA (Manchester)
Barrister, Hardwicke

Law Brief Publishing

Published 2018 by Law Brief Publishing, an imprint of Law Brief Publishing Ltd
30 The Parks
Minehead
Somerset
TA24 8BT

www.lawbriefpublishing.com

Paperback: 978-1-911035-56-5

PREFACE

It is an exciting time in the medico-legal sphere, with fast paced medical advancements and changing attitudes in society. Never more so than now has the law needed to be fluid in adapting to the challenges presented, and changes evoked, by the shifting socio-legal landscape.

I have long been passionate about the topics of wrongful conception, wrongful birth and wrongful life; they present an area of law in which a difficult balance must be struck between the competing needs to properly compensate claimants and to preserve the essential resources of the NHS. The question of the role of public policy considerations in legal decision-making is also at the forefront of these topics, making them all the more interesting. In writing this book I hoped to engage the reader with the issues presented by these areas of law, providing an in-depth look at the way in which the law has developed to date and an insight into the way it may yet develop further.

The contents of this book are current and accurate up to the date of completion of writing on 15 April 2018. It is my hope that a second edition will be necessary, the Supreme Court eventually re-examining these controversial areas of law and setting down principles which are more reflective of modern day attitudes, and responsive to modern day issues, than at present.

Whether you are a student, practitioner or interested member of the public, I hope you find this book interesting and informative, and as enjoyable to read as it has been to write.

Rebecca Greenstreet
April 2018

ACKNOWLEDGMENTS

With thanks to my parents, everyone at Law Brief Publishing and all of my colleagues and friends at Hardwicke, for their support and enthusiasm. Thanks also go to all those at Oxford University and Manchester University who inspired the content of this book.

Most of all I am grateful to Victor, my husband and chief proof-reader: thank you, for everything.

CONTENTS

CHAPTER ONE
AN INTRODUCTION TO THE CLAIMS

Objectives

This book provides an overview and analysis of the law in relation to wrongful life, wrongful conception and wrongful birth claims. After reading this book you will:

- Understand how to establish whether there is a cause of action in your cases in these areas.

- Have an in-depth understanding of the relevant case law, including a detailed working knowledge of the key judgments (detailed below).

- Be familiar with recent cases which have challenged those key judgments.

- Be aware of the way such claims have been treated in foreign jurisdictions.

- Have considered whether the principles laid down by the key cases ought to be re-visited by the Supreme Court and if so how best to challenge the established law.

The Different Claims

At the outset it is essential to understand the differences between the three types of claim.

- *Wrongful Life*: This type of claim is a case brought by a child who is alleging that but for the defendant's negligence they would never have been born and that that would have been a better outcome. English law does not currently recognise this type of case as a viable claim.

- *Wrongful Conception*: This is a claim brought where the negligence has resulted in a conception which the claimant had sought to avoid and normally arises out of a negligent sterilisation (whether it is a failed sterilisation operation or the incorrect provision of information regarding that operation).

- *Wrongful Birth*: Such cases are different to wrongful conception cases as here the claimants did not seek to avoid conception itself but instead the negligence has caused them to lose the opportunity to terminate a pregnancy (for example through negligent pre-natal screening). Interestingly such claims will often have the exact same factual matrix as wrongful life claims, despite the fact that English law does not currently recognise wrongful life claims as having a viable cause of action.

For wrongful conception and wrongful birth claims the recoverability of damages has proven controversial in English law. Any claim for the costs of bringing up a child (referred to throughout this book as maintenance costs) is currently not a recognised head of loss, with damages being restricted to those costs associated only with the pregnancy and birth and, as is explained later, for the extra maintenance costs which relate to a child's disability. It can also be argued that physical injury only arises in wrongful conception claims (as in wrongful birth claims the claimant already intended to become pregnant, whereas in wrongful conception claims this is what the claimants sought to avoid) and as such wrongful birth claims are claims for pure economic loss only.

The Established Case Law

There is only one key case in the United Kingdom in respect of wrongful life actions, *McKay v Essex Area Health Authority*[1]. The claimant here was a child who had been born disabled: the mother had

---

1 [1982] Q.B. 1166.

contracted rubella during pregnancy and it was alleged that but for the defendant's negligence the mother would have elected to have a termination and so the child would never have been born. The child's claim was for distress, loss and damage caused by having been brought in to a life in which she suffered from debilitating injuries. The Court of Appeal held that the child's claim was that the defendants had been negligent in allowing her to be born. The Court of Appeal dismissed that claim on the basis that it was contrary to public policy as a violation of the sanctity of life and that it was not possible to evaluate damages for the denial of non-existence.

The progression of the three key authorities in respect of the recovery of damages in wrongful conception and wrongful birth actions was as follows:

- *McFarlane v Tayside Health Board*[2]: The claimants decided they did not want any more children and so the husband underwent a vasectomy. Unfortunately following negligent advice as to the success of the operation the couple became parents to a healthy child. The House of Lords held that, although damages for the pain and suffering of pregnancy and childbirth could be awarded, the maintenance costs were irrecoverable.

- *Parkinson v St James and Seacroft University Hospital NHS Trust*[3]: This case presented a factual variation to *McFarlane*, where a child had been conceived and born due to negligent sterilisation but was not healthy as in *McFarlane* and instead was born with disabilities (such disabilities were not connected to the negligence). The Court of Appeal reiterated that any claim for the maintenance costs of a healthy child must fail but here allowed recovery of the extra costs associated with rearing a child with disabilities.

2 [2000] 2 A.C. 59.

3 [2001] EWCA Civ 530.

- *Rees v Darlington Memorial Hospital NHS Trust*[4]: The House of Lords was once again presented with a factual variation on the preceding cases, where here the claimant was a disabled woman who had elected to have a sterilisation operation because of the difficulties her disability would cause her in raising children. The sterilisation was performed negligently and resulted in the birth of a healthy child. The House of Lords determined that *Rees* was more in line with *McFarlane* than *Parkinson* and so the costs of rearing the child were irrecoverable, though a lump sum 'conventional award' of £15,000 was permitted to reflect the legal wrong suffered by the claimant.

The Current Position

There have been few cases decided in the UK since the above key judgments. There have been recent cases which have tested the boundaries of the principles set out by those key judgments, but none of these have rocked the boat in terms of the established law.

These cases have also been the subject of debate in foreign jurisdictions and an examination of the way in which this controversial topic has been dealt with across the globe provides an insight into the many different ways in which such claims are capable of being dealt with, with some foreign cases permitting wider recovery than is permitted by the UK courts.

There do still remain some unanswered questions as to the scope of recovery of damages in the United Kingdom, following the key judgments above, which include:

- The potential conflict between the denial of wrongful life actions by English courts and Section 1A(1)(b) of the *Congenital Disabilities (Civil Liability) Act 1976,* which permits a child to bring a claim for negligence during embryo selection which results in the claimant being born with a disability

4 [2004] 1 A.C. 309.

(which arguably amounts to a claim that the child would have been better off not being born and another healthier embryo having been selected instead).

- The extent to which the principles set out in *McFarlane*, *Parkinson* and *Rees* apply to wrongful birth cases: each of those key cases concerned wrongful conception claims and obiter comments in each suggested that wrongful birth claims prompted different policy considerations and so might be treated differently.

- The status of *Parkinson:* in *Rees* there was mixed judicial comment regarding the outcome in *Parkinson*.

- The rights of the father in such actions. Where the negligence in question occurs during the course of treatment / a procedure for the mother then the father's claim will be one purely for economic loss. This is different to where there is a negligent vasectomy (carried out on the father) which results in direct physical injury to the mother as well.

It is these areas which recent cases have explored and no doubt we will continue to see cases do so. The last major judgment in wrongful conception, wrongful birth or wrongful life claims was delivered over 15 years ago and so it is arguable that it is time for this controversial area of law to be re-visited by the Supreme Court.

CHAPTER TWO
IS THERE A CAUSE OF ACTION? DUTY, BREACH AND CAUSATION

Introduction

The most controversial aspect of wrongful conception and wrongful birth claims is the quantification of damages, however before examining the damages aspect of a claim it is necessary to establish whether there is an actionable claim in the first place. It should be noted, as will be explained in Chapter Three, English law does not presently recognise a cause of action for wrongful life claims: those cases where a child is bringing a claim themselves for damages relating to their own birth / life.[1]

There are three main questions which need to be asked when first assessing a claim: 1. Is a duty owed to the injured party? 2. Has this duty been breached? 3. Has the breach caused damage? If each of these questions can be answered in the affirmative, then there is a viable claim.

Is There a Duty?

The Parties to a Claim

Before determining whether a duty of care exists the parties to a claim need to be identified.

There may be more than one claimant and so each person who has suffered a loss as a result of alleged negligence needs to be considered. For example, in a wrongful conception case the father may be the

---

1 This is separate from those cases where negligence has caused a child to suffer disability, as opposed to causing the birth / life itself. There is no bar to these claims, which are permitted and dealt with under the *Congenital Disabilities (Civil Liability) Act 1976.*

person who has undergone the sterilisation treatment but, if performed negligently, the mother will also be affected as she will suffer a pregnancy and childbirth as a result of that negligence.

In cases where the father is the one who was sterilised or provided with advice, the mother's claim will usually be fairly straightforward as she has suffered a physical as well as a financial loss. However, there are still restrictions on when mothers are able to bring a claim as was shown in *Goodwill v British Pregnancy Advisory Service.* [2] *Goodwill* involved a claim for economic loss brought by a mother, who had fallen pregnant following a spontaneous reversal of a vasectomy which had been undertaken by her partner approximately three years prior to the onset of her relationship with him. The claim was struck out on appeal, as an abuse of process: the court held that at the time that the advice had been provided to the father the claimant mother was *"merely ... a member of an indeterminately large class of females who might have sexual relations"* with the father during his lifetime and as such the defendant could not be held to have voluntarily assumed responsibility towards the claimant, nor was the defendant in a sufficient or special relationship with her so as to give rise to a duty of care.[3]

Where the case involves a sterilisation of, or advice provided to, a mother then the father's position is less clear cut. He will need to establish a relationship of proximity to be able to bring a claim as the loss he has suffered is purely financial and so such loss must have been within the contemplation of the defendant at the time the negligence occurred. It is therefore important to examine the proximity of the relationship between the potential defendant and all potential claimants, whether the mother or the father, in such claims.

There may also be more than one defendant and so each of the individuals involved in the care of the potential claimant/s ought to identified and the treatment or advice which they provided carefully examined. As with assessing potential claimants, proximity will also need to be addressed when determining who the potential defendants to

---

2 [1996] 1 WLR 1397.

3 *Ibid.* at 1404 – 1405.

an action will be. In *Farraj v (1) Kings Healthcare NHS Trust and (2) Cytogenic DNA Services*[4] it was argued by the second defendant that they did not have a sufficient relationship of proximity to the claimant to be held liable. In this case the claimant and her husband had undergone DNA testing of their unborn child as both were carriers of a gene which could cause an inherited blood disorder and wished to detect whether the child would suffer from that disorder. Although the sample was taken by the first defendant it was sent to the second defendant, an independent laboratory, for testing to be undertaken. The test which was returned by the second defendant was negative but when the child was born it was found to be suffering from the genetic disorder. The Court of Appeal upheld the decision of the court at first instance, that there was a sufficient relationship of proximity between the claimant and the second defendant, since the second defendant had been aware of the purpose of the tests they were carrying out and ought to have been aware that parents in the claimants' position would rely on their skill and care in carrying out those tests.

As above it is not possible for a child to bring a wrongful life claim.[5] However, in these circumstances the facts will often be indistinguishable from wrongful birth actions (which are recognised under English Law) and so alternative claimants ought to be identified, such as the parents of the child.[6]

Tort

It is well established that a duty of care exists in the following scenarios:

---

4 [2006] EWHC 1228.

5 Wrongful life claims are dealt with in detail in Chapter Three. Children are able to bring claims under the *Congenital Disabilities (Civil Liability) Act 1976*, but these claims are separate and distinct from wrongful life actions.

6 Although see Wh*itehead v Searle* [2008] EWCA Civ 285 where a father was denied the right to bring a wrongful birth claim in place of the child, and where the mother had died and so could not bring the claim herself. This case is discussed more fully in Chapter Nine.

Wrongful Conception

- Sterilisation operations (see *Parkinson v St James and Seacroft University Hospital NHS Trust*[7] and *Rees v Darlington Memorial Hospital NHS Trust*[8]).

- Advice given in relation to sterilisation operations (*Newell v Goldenberg*[9] and *McFarlane v Tayside Health Board*[10]).

It can also be assumed that a claim could arise in relation to inaccurate testing following sterilisation operations. It is also possible that there may be a claim where there has been negligent provision of contraceptives or negligent contraceptive advice.[11]

Wrongful Birth

- Genetic counselling (*Lee v Taunton and Somerset NHS Trust*[12] *and Groom v Selby*[13]).[14]

---

7 [2001] EWCA Civ 530. Discussed in full in Chapter Six.

8 [2004] 1 A.C. 309. Discussed in full in Chapter Seven.

9 [1995] 6 Med. L.R. 371.

10 [2000] 2 A.C. 59. Discussed in full in Chapter Five.

11 See for example *Wooton v J Docter Ltd* [2008] EWC A Civ 1361, although in that case the claim was not made out it seems in principle that with different facts and levels of risks then similar claims might succeed.

12 [2001] 1 F.L.R. 419.

13 [2001] EWCA Civ 1522.

14 See also *ABC v St George's Healthcare NHS Foundation Trust* [2017] EWCA Civ 336 and *Smith v University of Leicester NHS Trust* [2016] EWHC 817: both cases address the extent to which a duty is owed to relatives of a patient, where information is known regarding the patient which might otherwise affect the reproductive choices of family members, such as the existence of hereditary conditions.

- Pre-natal testing (*Rand v East Dorset Health Authority*[15] and *Hardman v Amin*[16]).

It is also to be expected that a claim could be brought for negligence during IVF treatment, in line with claims for negligent pre-natal testing or genetic counselling.

Contract

There may also be a contractual cause of action, where for example the treatment is carried out in the private sector. Practically speaking there are no real differences between claims brought under contract and those brought under tort. Usually there will be an implied duty in a contract to exercise reasonable care and skill, which mirrors the duty which would be owed under tort, unless the contractual terms themselves impose a higher standard of care (which is very unlikely). *Thake v Maurice*[17] provides one such example. In that case the court would not imply a warranty that the sterilisation would be one hundred percent effective in to the contract but still found that there had been a breach of the implied duty to exercise reasonable care and skill.

The recent case of *ARB V IVF Hammersmith*[18] is an interesting example of how contractual duties can be relied on in the alternative to negligence as here, although the claimant's claim failed under both negligence and breach of the implied contractual duty to take reasonable care, the defendant was found to be strictly liable for breach of contract as the contract between the parties did not limit or exclude the relevant liability.

15 [2000] Lloyd's Rep. Med. 181.

16 [2000] Lloyd's Rep. Med. 498.

17 [1986] QB 644. Discussed in full in Chapter Four.

18 [2017] EWHC 2438 (Q.B.). Discussed in full in Chapter Nine.

Product Liability

There is also the possibility of bringing a product liability based wrongful conception claim following the failure of contraceptive methods. *Richardson v LRC*[19] concerned a claim brought under the *Consumer Protection Act 1987*[20] for an unwanted pregnancy, where a condom had split, and the claimant alleged that the condom was defective when it left the factory. Her case was dismissed on the grounds that she could not establish on her particular facts that the product was defective within the meaning of the *Consumer Protection Act 1987* but Kennedy J, delivering judgment, also found that the damages claim for maintenance costs was precluded by *McFarlane v Tayside Health Board*.[21] What is clear however is that it is possible in principle to bring a wrongful conception claim in cases which concern potentially defective products, such as contraceptive products or medicines, which result in an unwanted pregnancy or birth.

Has the Duty Been Breached?

Once it has been established that a duty of care exists then whether or not this duty has been breached must be examined. Even in contract the implied duty to exercise reasonable care and skill will be assessed by reference to usual tortious principles. The standard of care required will be assessed like any other clinical negligence claim, by reference to the tests set out in *Bolam v Friern Hospital Management Committee*,[22] *Bolitho v City & Hackney Health Authority*[23] and more recently *Montgomery v Lanarkshire Health Board*[24].

19 [2000] PIQR 164.

20 Which creates a strict liability for defective products.

21 [2000] 2 A.C. 59. Discussed in full in Chapter Five.

22 [1957] 2 All ER 118.

23 [1998] A.C. 232.

24 [2015] UKSC 11.

Bolam v Friern Hospital Management Committee

The longstanding test for the standard of care which is to be expected in a clinical setting was first set out in *Bolam*, which established the following principles for assessing whether there has been a breach of duty:

- A clinician will not be found negligent if he has *"acted in accordance with a practice accepted as proper by a responsible body of medical men skilled in that particular art."*[25]

- The burden of proof remains on the claimant.[26]

- The body of opinion does not need to be 'substantial' and provided that the defendant can point to a medical expert whose evidence is that the way he or she acted was acceptable then this will usually be enough. The defendant will be able to escape liability even if there is only a small number of practitioners who consider that he acted within the range of acceptable practices: in *Defreitas v O'Brien* even a number as small as only 11 specialists was held to be sufficient for the defendant to escape liability.[27]

- It is not for the court to weigh different bodies of expert opinion against one another and so if the defendant is supported by a medical expert then this will usually be enough for him or her to escape liability.[28]

- The standard of knowledge against which a medical practitioner is to be judged is that of a medical practitioner at the time the alleged negligence occurred and not with the benefit of hindsight.[29]

---

25 [1957] 1 W.L.R. 582 at 587.

26 *Defreitas v O'Brien* [1995] P.I.Q.R P281.

27 *Ibid.*

28 *Maynard v West Midlands Regional Health Authority* [1984] 1 WLR 634.

In practice this means that under the *Bolam* test claimants will have an uphill struggle to show that a defendant has acted negligently. *Bolam* made it clear that a defendant would not be found negligent *"merely because there is a body of opinion who would take a contrary view"* to him or her.[30] Thus, evidence will need to be called from an expert witness that no responsible body of medical opinion would have behaved as the defendant has done, rather than simply that that particular expert witness would not have done so.

Boltiho v City & Hackney Health Authority

The House of Lords re-examined *Bolam* in the case of *Bolitho.*[31] In *Bolitho*, with Lord Browne-Wilkinson delivering the lead judgment, it was held that although *Bolam* remained of 'central importance' in determining whether a doctor had been negligent the court was not bound to allow a defendant to escape from liability simply because that defendant had presented evidence from medical experts who believed that his or her actions conformed with acceptable medical practice. The reference to a 'responsible body of medical men' in *Bolam* meant that the court had to satisfy itself that the medical experts who supported the defendant's practices had a logical basis for their opinion; it would however be rare for the court to reject the medical experts' views as unreasonable.[32]

Bolitho thus challenged the conventional approach under *Bolam*, with it appearing from Lord Browne-Wilkinson's judgment that the court should play a more proactive role in examining the bodies of professional opinion presented in clinical negligence cases. It was generally accepted in subsequent cases that *Bolitho* presented a qualification to the test as set out in *Bolam*. We can therefore expect courts to scrutinise

29 *Roe v Ministry of Health* [1954] 2 Q.B. 66 at 84.

30 [1957] 1 W.L.R. 582 at 587.

31 [1998] A.C. 232.

32 [1998] A.C. 232 at 241 – 243. For an example of a recent wrongful birth case in which the *Bolam* and *Bolitho* tests were applied see *McGuinn v Lewisham and Greenwich NHS Trust* [2017] EWHC 88 (QB).

expert medical evidence more closely following *Bolitho*, though only in appropriate cases will courts find a body of medical opinion to be illogical or indefensible. Even if it is expected to be rare, where a court is not satisfied by the expert medical evidence of the defendant, *Bolitho* makes possible a finding of negligence against that defendant, even where he or she has led expert evidence in support of their actions.[33]

Montgomery v Lanarkshire Health Board

There are slightly different additional considerations involved when addressing whether there has been a breach of duty in providing information and obtaining informed consent. The Supreme Court revisited the question of consent in the case of *Montgomery*.[34] In *Montgomery* it was held that when obtaining consent the correct legal test in establishing the extent of a duty is as follows:[35]

---

33 It is outside the scope of this book to thoroughly analyse the subsequent application of the *Bolam* / *Bolitho* tests by courts. For further information see for example *Smith v Southampton University Hospitals NHS Trust* [2007] EWCA Civ 387; *Gouldsmith v Mid-Staffordshire General Hospitals NHS Trust* [2007] EWCA Civ 397; *Burne v A* [2006] EWCA Civ 24; *Muller v King's College Hospital NHS Foundation Trust* [2017] EWHC 128 (QB); *Hearne v Royal Marsden Hospital NHS Foundation Trust* [2016] EWHC 117 (QB); *XYZ v Warrington and Halton NHS Foundation Trust* [2016] EWHC 331 (QB); *Ecclestone v Medway NHS Foundation Trust* [2013] EWHC 790 (QB).

34 [2015] UKSC 11. The extent of the duty of care when providing information and obtaining informed consent had already been considered in the two cases of *Sidaway v Board of Governors of the Bethlehem Royal Hospital* [1985] A.C. 871 and *Pearce v United Bristol Healthcare NHS Trust* [1999] PIQR P53 (which extended the *Bolam* test to cases involving the provision of information and informed consent). As *Montgomery* was re-visiting *Sidaway*, an earlier House of Lords decision, it came before a 7-member Supreme Court which ultimately found the reasoning in *Sidaway* to be unsatisfactory for present day purposes.

35 [2015] UKSC 11 at [68] – [93] and [108].

- The doctor is under a duty to take reasonable care to ensure that the patient is aware of any material risks involved in any recommended treatment, and of any reasonable alternative or variant treatments.

- Materiality is assessed as follows:

  - By establishing whether, in the circumstances of the particular case, a reasonable person in the patient's position would be likely to attach significance to the risk, or the doctor is or should reasonably be aware that the particular patient would be likely to attach significance to it.

  - Materiality does not depend on the percentage of risk, and the significance of a risk is likely to reflect a variety of factors besides its magnitude, including the nature and the consequences of the risk, the importance of the treatment results, the alternatives and the risks associated with those.

  - Assessing materiality is a fact sensitive exercise.

- Patient autonomy is of paramount importance.

A v East Kent Hospitals University NHS Foundation Trust[36] is a recent example of a post-*Montgomery* wrongful birth case in which the court found that there had been no breach of duty.[37] The claimant alleged that the defendant had failed to advise her that her baby might be suffering from a chromosomal abnormality and that had she been so advised she would have undergone further investigations, these would

---

36 [2015] EWHC 1038 (QB).

37 To compare to a pre-*Montgomery* wrongful birth case see *Schumann v Veale Wasbrough*, also known as *Chinnock v Veale Wasbrough* [2015] EWCA Civ 441.

have revealed the abnormality and she would have then terminated her pregnancy (albeit at a late stage of between 32-35 weeks).[38]

Dingemans J heard the claim on liability only and delivered judgment rejecting the claimant's claim. First, he held that the risk of the claimant's baby suffering from a chromosomal abnormality was not material but was no more than background level.[39] Considering *Montgomery* he held that it was not *"authority for the proposition that medical practitioners need to warn about risks which are theoretical and not material."*[40] He further did not consider it likely that, in light of the level of the risk of the child suffering from an abnormality, that the claimant would have in fact even undergone further investigations such as an amniocentesis.[41] Accordingly he dismissed the claim.[42]

Causation

Even once the existence and breach of a duty has been established, that is not the end of matters and it must be determined whether the breach of duty in question has caused foreseeable damage or loss. If causation cannot be satisfied, then the claim will fail.

Deriche v Ealing Hospital NHS Trust[43] provides a good example of the types of cases in which a claimant's case will fail at the causation hurdle. In this case the claimant alleged that her consultant obstetrician had been negligent in failing to fully advise her of the risks to her unborn

---

38 [2015] EWHC 1038 (QB) at [1].

39 *Ibid.* at [84] – [91].

40 *Ibid.* at [90].

41 *Ibid.* at [92] – [96].

42 *Ibid.* at [101] – [102]. Dingemans J also dismissed the claim on the basis that he did not consider it likely that the claimant would have elected to undergo a termination even if she had been provided with the information, as is discussed below.

43 [2003] EWHC 3104.

child associated with her having contracted chicken pox during pregnancy. Although it was held that the consultant had indeed been negligent in failing to properly advise the claimant, her claim was still dismissed on the grounds that causation had not been established. The claimant had also received advice from a registrar as to the risks and had not then immediately opted for a termination, instead accepting the 'small risk'; had the consultant advised her of the risks he would have only been expressly confirming the earlier advice of the registrar and there was no basis for finding that the claimant's reaction to his advice would have been any different.

The case of *Lillywhite v University College London Hospitals' NHS Trust* presented a case where the claimant was able to make out causation.[44] Here the claimant brought a claim following the failure of a specialist consultant to identify fetal brain abnormalities when performing an ultrasound: in fact the consultant identified three relevant structures of the brain as present when they were not. He was therefore found to have breached his duty.[45] The claimant was able to satisfy the court as to causation as she had taken steps to obtain further opinions as to the risk of her child being born with a disability; the court accepted her evidence that had she been informed of the fetal brain abnormalities then she would have sought a termination.

---

44 [2005] EWCA Civ 1466.

45 Interesting questions also arise as to the applicability of the doctrine of *res ipsa loquitur* to wrongful conception and wrongful birth cases, which are outside the scope of this book. It is however worth noting that in *Lillywhite* the Court of Appeal held that the doctrine would rarely be useful when the court had heard full and detailed evidence from all of the parties. In this case they found that the errors which the claimant had identified in the consultant's performance of the ultrasound scan meant that the court needed to carefully focus on the explanation provided by the consultant to try and displace the inference from the claimant's evidence that he had not acted with reasonable care and skill: they were able to make a finding of negligence without relying on the 'special doctrine' of *res ipsa loquitur.*

The case of *A v East Kent Hospitals University NHS Foundation Trust*[46] also presented a causation issue. Although Dingemans J would have dismissed the case on the basis that there had been no breach of duty in any event he also considered that the claimant faced a causation hurdle; he held that even if the claimant had been informed of the risk of chromosomal abnormality and even if she had undergone further investigations she still would not have elected to undergo a termination, and would have *"continued with, the pregnancy hoping for the best outcome"*. This was enough to bar recovery and dismiss her claim.[47]

In wrongful conception cases it is important to establish exactly when the claimant's knowledge of the failed sterilisation arose and whether they continued to engage in unprotected sexual intercourse thereafter. It will obviously amount to a break in the chain in causation if the claimant knew of the fact of a failure (or the risk of one) and nevertheless continued to engage in unprotected sexual intercourse. In *Sabri-Tabrizi v Lothian Health Board* the claimant underwent a sterilisation procedure which was performed negligently, following which she became pregnant and underwent a termination.[48] However following that termination the claimant went on to become pregnant again and she then brought a claim against the defendant. Her claim was dismissed, and it was held that following her termination she was aware of the risk of becoming pregnant, and it was not reasonable for the claimant to have exposed herself to that risk: her decision to do so thereby constituted a break in the chain of causation.

Claimants in wrongful birth and wrongful conception cases are also under a duty to mitigate their loss like any other claimant. However, it is now well established that if a claimant in a wrongful conception or wrongful birth case elects not to undergo a termination or elects not to exercise the right to have their child adopted then those choices will not amount to a failure to mitigate. In light of this and considering the limited heads of loss which can currently be claimed in such cases, there

---

46 [2015] EWHC 1038 (QB) and discussed above regarding breach of duty.

47 *Ibid.* at [97] – [100] and [102].

48 1998 S.C. 373.

are therefore presently very few, if any, circumstances one can envisage where an argument that the claimant has failed to mitigate their loss would be successful in reducing the damages claimed.

Summary

In order for there to be a viable claim the following criteria have to be established:

1. Does a duty of care exist?
2. Has that duty been breached?
3. Has the breach of duty caused damage / loss?

In order to satisfy each of those questions the parties to any potential action need to be identified as well as the grounds on which any claim can be made. Whether or not a duty exists will depend on the facts of each case and whether there has been a breach will depend on the application of normal tortious or contractual principles. The availability of clinical guidance may also be a useful aide when determining whether there has been a breach early on in a case.[49] As usual causation will also need to be carefully examined. Once the above have been satisfied then quantification of the loss which has been suffered follows. It is at this stage when matters become more controversial in wrongful conception and wrongful birth cases: the historical approach to the measure of damages, as well as recent developments in the law governing such loss, is examined in the remainder of this book.

49 See for example advice provided by the Royal College of Obstetricians and Gynaecologists (RCOG) (last updated in 2004) at https://www.rcog.org.uk/globalassets/documents/patients/patient-information-leaflets/gynaecology/sterilisation-for-women-and-men.pdf; See also family planning information referred to by RCOG at https://www.fpa.org.uk/sites/default/files/male-and-female-sterilisation-your-guide.pdf

CHAPTER THREE
WRONGFUL LIFE

Introduction

A wrongful life claim is a claim brought by a child who has been born with disabilities, alleging that but for some negligence during the mother's pregnancy that pregnancy would have been terminated and the child would never have been born. The damage being claimed is that that child's own life should have been avoided.

English law does not currently recognise wrongful life claims as having a valid cause of action. There is only one leading English authority on wrongful life claims, *McKay v Essex Area Health Authority and Another.*[1] In *McKay* a claim was brought by a child, who was born with disabilities following an alleged failure by clinicians to identify exposure to rubella in utero and to offer her mother a termination. The child claimed for damages for the distress and suffering her life with disabilities caused. The claim was identified as a wrongful life claim by the Court of Appeal and was struck out as disclosing no reasonable cause of action.

The Facts

McKay concerned a claim brought both by a child and her mother. The mother had suffered from an infection of rubella during her pregnancy and as a result the child was born with deformities. During her pregnancy the mother had sought advice from her doctor, who had sent a blood sample for testing but communicated to the mother that she had no infection. It was alleged that but for the negligence in identifying the rubella infection the mother would have undergone an abortion and the child would never have been born.

Both the mother and the child brought a claim for damages. The mother's claim was that but for the negligence of the defendants she

1 [1982] Q.B. 1166.

would have undergone an abortion to terminate her pregnancy. The child's claim was first against the doctor for failing to treat the rubella and second against both of the defendants on the basis that as a result of their negligence she had *"suffered entry into a life in which her injuries are highly debilitating"* and distress, loss and damage.[2]

The case first came before the court on a strike out application made by the defendants against all but one of the child's claims. All of the claims made by the mother and the claim made by the child against the doctor, for failing to treat the rubella, were to continue regardless of the outcome of the strike out application. The court therefore only had to determine whether the child had a cause of action for *"being allowed to enter life damaged – what has been called 'wrongful life'"* or whether her claims in this regard ought to be struck out.[3]

The Decisions of the Lower Courts

Master Bickford-Smith originally heard the strike out application. He agreed with the defendants and struck out the claim on the basis that it disclosed no reasonable cause of action.

On appeal the application was heard by Lawson J who overturned the decision of the Master. He considered that the child's claim was not a complaint that she had been born but was a complaint that she had been born with deformities. He held that the child's case presented *"a highly reasonable and arguable cause of action."*[4]

That decision was then appealed by the defendants and the case came before the Court of Appeal.

2 *Ibid.*

3 *Ibid.* at 1175.

4 *Ibid.*

The Decision of the Court of Appeal

The Court of Appeal rejected any claim for wrongful life, holding that the claim brought by the child disclosed no reasonable cause of action and was not a valid claim under English law. Stephenson LJ delivered the lead judgment and made the following findings:

- The basis of the child's claim was that the defendants were negligent in allowing her to be born and was accordingly a 'wrongful life' claim[5]:

    - The child would have a claim against the defendants had she been injured as a result of the defendants breaching a duty to take reasonable care of her but here the child *"has not been injured by either defendant, but by the rubella which has infected the mother without fault on anybody's part."*

    - The disabilities of the child had not been caused by any act or omission of the defendants and so her right not to be injured by others had not been infringed.

    - The right which the child relied on as having been infringed was therefore a right not to be born disabled: for a child who suffered disability in the womb this amounted to a right not to be born at all (which was also a right to be aborted or killed).

- There was no duty owed to a child to provide its mother with the opportunity of a termination, as this would violate the sanctity of human life and was contrary to public policy[6]:

    - The *Abortion Act 1967* provided an *"inroad on the sanctity of life by recognising that it would be better for a*

5 *Ibid.* at 1178 – 1179.

6 *Ibid.* at 1179 – 1180.

child, born to suffer from such abnormalities as to be seriously handicapped, not to have been born at all". However, the act did not create a legal obligation towards a foetus to terminate its life.

    - Although the defendants were under a duty to advise the mother of her right to a termination and provide her with the opportunity to undergo the same, that duty did not extend to the child.

    - To hold that such a duty existed would *"make a further inroad on the sanctity of human life which would be contrary to public policy."*

    - If such a duty existed then it would also be possible for children to bring claims against their mothers for failing to undergo an abortion.

- The effect of the *Congenital Disabilities (Civil Liability) Act 1976* was that no child born after the passing of the act would have a cause of action based on the loss of a chance to die. The act was worded so *"as to import the assumption that but for the occurrence giving rise to a disabled birth, the child would have been born normal and healthy – not that it would not have been born at all."*[7]

- The court could not evaluate the damages claimed in any event[8]:

    - One way to calculate damages would be to pay for the difference between a healthy life and an injured life, but this would treat the defendants as if they had injured the child when they did not.

---

7 *Ibid.* at 1178 and 1186 – 1187.

8 *Ibid.* at 1181 – 1182.

  - The other, more accurate, way of calculating damages would be to calculate the difference between living and never having been born, but it is impossible for the court to assess such loss.

  - The problem encountered by courts in attempting to compare existence to non-existence was not the same as the difficulty courts are used to encountering when assessing damages.

  - It is not possible for the court to place a monetary value on the loss of an expectation of death and *"if difficulty in assessing damages is a bad reason for refusing the task, impossibility of assessing them is a good one."*

- If the court had to decide whether it was better to be born with disabilities or not to be born at all then it would be bound to find that, in all but exceptional cases, it was better to be born. However, it was not for the court to engage in such a balancing exercise.[9]

- The court was considering a novel cause of action, for which there was no authority in the courts of the United Kingdom or the Commonwealth. There were some cases from the United States of America and all but one had denied claims for wrongful life.[10]

Ackner LJ and Griffiths LJ also delivered short judgments, agreeing with the reasoning of Stephenson LJ in denying the wrongful life claim.

Ackner LJ agreed with Stephenson LJ on the following points[11]:

---

9 *Ibid.* at 1182.

10 *Ibid.* at 1177 and 1182 – 1184.

11 *Ibid.* at 1188 – 1189.

- The effect of the *Congenital Disabilities (Civil Liability) Act 1976* in denying wrongful life claims.

- That there was no duty owed to a foetus to provide the opportunity of a termination.

- That such a duty was contrary to the sanctity of life.

- To allow a claim like the child's in *McKay* would open the door to claims against a mother or by children with only minor disabilities.

- That compensation would be based on a comparison between the value of non-existence and existence in a disabled state, which it was not possible to undertake.

Griffiths LJ provided a dissent but only in respect of whether the issue was one which was appropriate for strike out (he considered that it ought to have been determined at trial but nonetheless would have found the claim to be invalid).[12] He considered that wrongful life actions were not valid and his main reasons for so finding were the impossibility of assessing the damage the child has suffered and the difficulties with determining how disabled a child would need to be before the bringing of such a claim was appropriate.[13]

It is worth noting that the court only has a discretion to strike out claims in 'plain and obvious' cases and so Stephenson LJ and Ackner LJ clearly were both of the opinion that, not only did wrongful life claims not present a valid cause of action, but that this was so clear cut as to satisfy the 'plain and obvious' criteria.

---

12 *Ibid.* at 1189 – 1191.

13 *Ibid.* at 1192 – 1193.

Summary

The judgment of the Court of Appeal in *McKay* was unanimous: wrongful life claims could not be validly brought under English law. *McKay* thus established that there was no cause of action for 'wrongful life' and that children suffering from deformities would not be able to bring a claim against a defendant for allowing them to be born.

The outcome of *McKay* means that a child will not be able to bring a claim for damages in their own right. However, the facts in wrongful life claims will often be indistinguishable from wrongful birth claims and so the mother in such cases will be able to bring a claim for damages and receive some limited compensation to go towards the maintenance costs associated with the upbringing of a disabled child.[14] Difficulties might however arise where the child is not able to obtain such compensation from their mother, for example where they have been cared for by someone else or where the mother has died.[15] The fact that the mother in these cases often will be able to bring a valid (wrongful birth) claim for damages does weaken the reasoning in *McKay* that the child's claim ought to be rejected due to the impossib-ility in calculating damages: the loss claimed by the mother is the exact same loss claimed by the child and is clearly capable of assessment in the mother's case. [16]

The decision in *McKay* does not affect the right of a child to bring a statutory claim for damages where they have been injured in utero due to negligence and are consequently born with disabilities, pursuant to the *Congenital Disabilities (Civil Liability) Act 1976*. These claims differ

---

14 Discussed further in Chapter Six.

15 See *Whitehead v Searle* [2008] EWCA Civ 285 for an example of this in action, also discussed in ChapterNine.

16 See wrongful birth claims *Rand v East Dorset Health Authority* [2000] Lloyd's Med Rep 181, *Hardman v Amin* [2000] Lloyd's Med Rep 498, *Lee v Taunton and Somerset NHS Trust,* [2001] FLR 419. These cases are also discussed in Chapter Six.

from wrongful life claims as they will concern disabilities which are caused by an act or omission of a defendant and the pleaded claim is likely to be that but for the negligence they would have been born normal and healthy (as opposed to wrongful life claims where the pleaded claim is that but for the negligence the child would not have been born at all). There is now some conflict between the outcome in *McKay* and the wording of Section 1A(1)(b) of the *Congenital Disabilities (Civil Liability) Act 1976* (Section 1A was inserted by way of the *Human Fertilisation and Embryology Act 1990* which was brought in to force years after the judgment in *McKay*). That sub-section now makes it possible for a claim to be brought for negligence in the selection of embryos: it is difficult to see how such a claim would be consistent with an outright denial of wrongful life actions since undoubtedly one of the allegations from a child bringing a claim under Section 1A(1)(b) would be that the embryo from which they grew should not have been selected (and so they should never have been born).

There has been no challenge to the judgment in *McKay* in the 35 years since it was delivered. The law governing wrongful life claims has therefore remained the same, notwithstanding the above and that recent wrongful conception and wrongful birth claims and those concerning end of life decisions have thrown some of the reasoning in *McKay* under the microscope. Recent developments and changes in the law which might have some impact on wrongful life claims are discussed in Chapters Eight, Eleven and Thirteen.

CHAPTER FOUR
WRONGFUL CONCEPTION AND WRONGFUL BIRTH: THE BACKGROUND

Introduction

McFarlane v Tayside Health Board[1] is the leading case concerning the recoverability of damages for maintenance costs in wrongful birth and wrongful conception cases.[2] It is important to understand the background to the decision in *McFarlane* and so the progression of English law prior to *McFarlane* warrants close examination. This chapter takes an in depth look at the cases immediately preceding the decision in *McFarlane* and examines the reasons behind the decision of the House of Lords. Were the recoverability of maintenance costs to be re-visited by the Supreme Court in the future then these old cases provide us with lessons to be learned, to ensure that future cases promote consistency and fairness in relation to this difficult head of damages.

Udale v Bloomsbury Area Health Authority: Rejecting the Recovery of Maintenance Costs

Udale v Bloomsbury Area Health Authority[3] provided an early example of those factors which can operate on judicial decision making in this controversial area.

Udale concerned a claim brought following a negligent sterilisation operation, resulting in the conception and birth of a healthy, though unwanted, baby. Liability was admitted but the quantum of damages disputed. The damages sought included claims for pain and discomfort,

1 [2000] 2 A.C. 59.

2 *McFarlane* and the key cases which followed it are covered in detail in Chapters Five, Six and Seven.

3 [1983] 1 WLR 1098.

loss of earnings, maintenance costs of the child until the age of 16 and a claim for the cost of enlarging the family home in order to accommodate the growing family.[4]

Jupp J allowed only part of the claim, awarding damages for the loss of earnings during pregnancy and to reflect the pain and suffering of pregnancy and childbirth. He did not consider it appropriate to make an award of damages for maintenance costs or for enlarging the family home and so rejected those parts of the claim on the grounds of public policy.[5]

Jupp J did consider that any damages awarded should reflect the *"significant financial disruption caused by pregnancy"* but regarded the subsequent financial disruption of raising a child as outside of recovery. Instead he recognised the *"disturbance to the family finances"* caused by the conception and birth, by increasing the general damages award. This of course in no meaningful way compensated for the costs of a child's upbringing but was a recognition, even in a case where maintenance costs were rejected, that there had been a wrong suffered by the claimant which would represent a financial loss to her.

The main policy concerns operating in *Udale* were listed by Jupp J as follows[6]:

- That there was a risk of disrupting the social concept of family life: it was undesirable that any child ever learn that a court had *"publicly declared his or her life or birth to be a mistake."*

- That *"virtue would go unrewarded,"* since damages would be offset against any joy demonstrated by parents at the birth of a child and so those parents who demonstrated bitterness would be entitled to higher damages awards.

---

4 *Ibid.* at 1099.

5 *Ibid.* at 1098.

6 *Ibid.* at 1109.

- That there would be a change in the way pregnancy was treated by clinicians, with a pressure to encourage abortions so as to avoid expensive medical negligence claims.

- That viewing a child as a source of dismay rather than joy would have a negative impact on the sanctity of life: life was a blessing and not something which should be compensated for.

Jupp J also relied on the earlier case of *McKay v Essex Area Health Authority*, a wrongful life case,[7] in support of these policy considerations.[8] While accepting that *McKay* involved a wrongful life claim which distinguished it from the facts in *Udale*, Jupp J believed it illustrated how policy considerations should be given weight in this area of law.[9]

Jupp J was transparent in his reasoning, explicitly acknowledging that public policy heavily informed his decision to reject maintenance costs. It does not appear however that Jupp J engaged with the impact a blanket denial on recovery of maintenance costs would have on claimants: at one point in his judgment Jupp J poses the question as to whether the birth of a happy healthy boy was fortunate or unfortunate, concluding that where a healthy child is born then such a birth will always be seen as fortunate.[10] Such a conclusion appears to have been drawn without regard to the fact that, irrespective of the health of the child and whether the parents were now happy and the baby now loved, this was a birth which the parents had not wanted and which would not have occurred but for the defendant's negligence.

---

7 Discussed more fully in Chapter Three.

8 *Udale v Bloomsbury Area Health* Authority [1983] 1 WLR 1098 at 1109.

9 *Ibid.* at 1108.

10 *Ibid.* at 1109.

Thake v Maurice: permitting the recovery of maintenance costs (but not in all cases?)

Jupp J's commitment to the importance of public policy in wrongful birth and wrongful conception cases set out in *Udale* did not go unchallenged. *Thake v Maurice*[11] was a breach of contract claim brought against a private hospital, in which the claimant alleged that there had been a failure to properly warn of the risk of a vasectomy reversing. The Court of Appeal held that there had been a breach of the contractual duty of care, sufficient to amount to negligence in contract and in tort. In quantifying damages, the Court of Appeal held that there was no public policy rule preventing the recovery of damages for the consequent conception and birth of a healthy baby.[12]

Although *Thake* was a contractual claim the judgement of Peter Pain J at first instance, which was affirmed by the Court of Appeal, is of particular importance because of his thorough analysis of public policy considerations.[13] The public policy arguments against permitting recovery of damages in *Udale* were considered in turn by Peter Pain J, and each rejected for lack of strength[14]:

- He considered that any negative impact on a child of learning that their birth was unplanned was counter-acted by the love and support provided to that child even in the face of financial difficulty.

- Although he considered the difficulty with calculations seeking to offset the benefits of a child from the cost of bringing up a child, he thought it necessary to separate the consideration of financial elements from intangible ones.

11 *Thake v Maurice* [1986] Q.B. 644.

12 *Ibid.*

13 *Ibid.* at 666.

14 *Ibid.* at 666 – 668.

- He also held that just because the child had been welcomed into a household with love and joy did not mean that this should be offset against the financial disadvantage; it was to the credit of the parents that they had made good of the situation in which they found themselves but that did not reduce their financial burden.

- He was not persuaded that permitting such claims would lead to clinicians encouraging abortions.

- In respect of the need to regard a healthy baby as a blessing, he held that the availability of family planning options illustrated that with time the notion of a family had moved on in recognition of the fact that a child was not always something that was sought after.

- He also held that although it was true that a healthy baby was normally an occasion for joy this same baby still *"has a belly to be filled and a body to be clothed."*

- He drew attention to the fact that if claimants in wrongful conception and wrongful birth cases viewed their child as a blessing then they would not have undergone the procedures in question in the first place, in this way engaged with the balancing exercise that Jupp J did not undertake in *Udale*.

Thake represented a strong rebuttal of Jupp J's support for public policy in *Udale*, taking a pragmatic approach to the issue of maintenance costs. Many of the arguments employed by Peter Pain J in *Thake* were mirrored in the later Australian case of *Cattanach v Melchior.*[15]

The Court of Appeal in *Thake*, despite denying public policy influence and affirming Peter Pain J's decision, did concede that it might intervene to deny recovery in other cases, without specifically indicating what change in factual circumstances might permit this. The judgment

15 See Chapters Eleven and Twelve for a full discussion of case law from other jurisdictions.

of the Court of Appeal also failed to define the scope of recovery of maintenance costs, making no determination as to the limits of recovery generally and therefore leaving those to subsequent courts to define. *Thake* therefore represents a missed opportunity to fine tune the beginnings of a logical and coherent approach to recoverable maintenance costs and continued to leave the debate open.

Emeh v Kensington Area Health Authority (Issues of Causation / Failure to Mitigate)

The Court of Appeal also considered whether maintenance costs should be recoverable in *Emeh v Kensington Health Authority,*[16] the decision coming after Peter Pain J's first instance judgment in *Thake* but prior to the Court of Appeal in *Thake* hearing the issue. *Emeh* involved a case where a negligent sterilisation had resulted in the conception of a child suffering from congenital disabilities, which were not a direct consequence of the negligence itself.[17]

At first instance Park J held that the claimant was entitled to no damages following her discovery of her pregnancy, due to her failure to have an abortion from this point. The Court of Appeal reversed Park J's first instance decision to bar recovery, and rejected the argument by counsel for the defendant that any damages should be reduced in recognition of *Udale.*[18] Maintenance costs were held to be recoverable, as avoiding pregnancy had been the object of the sterilisation operation and any financial loss flowed directly from the negligence. Park J's assertion that the claimant was under a duty to mitigate her own loss through having an abortion was also firmly rejected. [19]

The Court of Appeal judgments were as follows:

16 [1985] Q.B. 1012.

17 *Ibid.*

18 *Ibid.*

19 *Ibid.*

- Waller LJ rejected any argument that damages ought to be denied on the grounds of public policy. He was insufficiently persuaded by the treatment of cases in other jurisdictions and in the UK, *Udale* included.[20] Citing *McLoughlin v Brian,* a case not related to the current facts but one which demonstrated how policy factors should impact any judicial decision making, he held that *"policy considerations will have to be weighed: but the objective of the judges is the formulation of principle."*[21] He went on to make clear that if adjudicating on principle resulted in an outcome that was socially unacceptable or entailed policy risk then Parliament could intervene and legislate, but that policy curtailment was not to be a function of the courts.[22]

- Slade LJ compared the arguments put forward by Jupp J in *Udale* (in favour of relying on public policy) and Peter Pain J in *Thake* (against relying on public policy), preferring the reasoning of the latter.[23] He held that the loss suffered by the claimant was reasonable foreseeable financial loss caused by the unexpected pregnancy, which included the obvious fact that a child might be conceived and born to individuals who did not want to be parents and who were now subject to the significant financial burden of raising that child.[24] He also held that *"save in the most exceptional circumstances"* it would never be unreasonable for a woman to decline to have an abortion.

- Purchas LJ held that denying maintenance costs created a qualification to "*the perfectly ordinary, straightforward rules of recovery of damages,*" something which should not be a change that the

20 *Ibid.* at 1021.

21 *McLoughlin v O'Brian* [1983] 1 A.C. 410; *Ibid.*

22 *Emeh v Kensington and Chelsea Area Health Authority* [1985] Q.B. 1012 at 1021.

23 *Ibid.* at 1025.

24 *Ibid.* at 1023.

> court invokes unless directed to do so by Parliament.[25] He held that where damage can be shown as caused by negligence and this is both reasonable and not remote then it should be recoverable.[26]

Emeh therefore firmly rejected the influence of public policy, with the Court of Appeal affirming that the normal principles of recovery in tort should apply for wrongful conception or wrongful birth cases, including permitting an award for maintenance costs.[27] *Emeh*, despite being a case concerning a child born with disabilities, applied to all children including the healthy and as such overturned *Udale*, becoming the leading UK authority on this area of law prior to *McFarlane*.[28]

A Difficult Application in Subsequent Cases

Problems with the scope and extent of recovery of maintenance costs in wrongful conception and wrongful birth cases were quickly identified by subsequent courts, which struggled to place appropriate parameters on this new head of loss.[29]

Benarr v Kettering: Is Private Education a Maintenance Cost?

Benarr v Kettering,[30] although a case which pre-dates *Emeh*, provides a good example of the type of difficulty subsequent courts faced when

---

25 *Ibid.* at 1028.

26 *Ibid.* at 1029.

27 Which would remain the case until *McFarlane v Tayside Health Board* [2000] 2 A.C. 59 came before the House of Lords; Discussed in detail in Chapter Five.

28 *Emeh v Kensington and Chelsea Area Health Authority* [1985] Q.B. 1012.

29 *Walkin v South Manchester Health Authority* [1995] 1 WLR 1543; *Allen v Bloomsbury Health Authority* [1992] P.I.Q.R. Q50; *Goodwill v British Pregnancy Advisory Service* [1996] 1 WLR 1397; *Salih v Enfield* [1991] 3 All ER 400; *Benarr v Kettering* (1988) 138 N.L.J. 179.

30 (1988) 138 N.L.J. 179.

attempting to define the extent of recovery of maintenance costs. In *Benarr* the costs of privately educating a child were accepted as a proper and ordinary feature of the family and as such were eligible for inclusion in an award for maintenance costs, despite the significant increase in damages this would entail.[31]

There are obvious difficulties with an approach permitting recovery of maintenance costs without setting adequate parameters, the most troubling of which is without doubt the financial and administrative burden which would be placed on the National Health Service and clinicians were all-inclusive and unlimited awards permitted.[32] However strictly following the ordinary principles of tort requires restorative damages: this means awarding damages for any expense which would not have been accrued but for the negligence. In *Benarr* the claimants had demonstrated that private education would be an expense they would incur for all of their children (including the child born of negligence), thus private education for the child born of negligence was an expense which would not have arisen but for that negligence and the parents ought to be compensated for the same.

Although, as was acknowledged in *Emeh*, the financial burden of child rearing is a reasonably foreseeable one, there are clear problems with permitting an unlimited category of expenses to be included in such loss. These include:

- The open-ended nature of this type of assessment increases the lack of consistency and predictability in the types and amounts of damages awards being made in such cases.

- The criteria that costs should be ordinary and proper features of each particular family might permit the inclusion of non-essential maintenance costs and provides no guidance for those cases involving claimants who have not had children previously.

31 *Ibid.*

32 This was one of Jupp J's own policy concerns in *Udale v Bloomsbury Area Health Authority* [1983] 1 WLR 1098 and similar concerns can be seen operating in the judgments of *McFarlane v Tayside Health Board* [2000] 2 A.C. 59.

- *Benarr* also illustrates how a wholly subjective assessment of maintenance costs could lead to variations according to the socio-economic status of claimants, with the wealthier claimants being eligible for significantly larger awards and struggling families who had only been able to provide the bare minimum in the past being eligible for less.[33]

Salih v Enfield: The Risk of Over-Compensating

Subsequent courts also encountered problems with causation of loss, and limiting maintenance costs accordingly. *Salih v Enfield*[34] is one such example, where negligence occurred which prevented the claimant from being able to choose an abortion; the child was born severely handicapped and it was the claimant's evidence that had she been given the opportunity she would have terminated a handicapped foetus.[35]

Although acknowledging that the negligence of the clinician had resulted in a lost opportunity to terminate the pregnancy, full damages for the maintenance of the consequent child were not awarded on the basis that had the claimant terminated that pregnancy she still would have gone on to become pregnant again.[36] Instead, the court deducted the cost of raising a healthy child from the damages in recognition that the claimants were trying to conceive and raise a child in the first place, and as such the financial consequence of negligence was reflected in the additional costs of raising a handicapped child instead of a healthy one.[37]

Even if at first blush the decision in *Salih* appears unfair, such a decision holds logical appeal given that the costs of raising a child were not something which the claimants would have otherwise escaped; this is

---

33 (1988) 138 N.L.J. 179.

34 [1991] 3 All ER 400.

35 *Ibid.*

36 *Ibid.*

37 *Ibid.*

not the same scenario as *McFarlane* where the claimants were attempting to protect themselves forever from those costs. It is however arguable that the court in *Salih* took an overly simplistic approach by simply deducting the maintenance costs of a healthy child from the damages awarded. One might wonder what would have happened were the claimants in *Salih* only able to afford one child: the negligence they suffered has then deprived them of the opportunity to raise a healthy child since they have still had to pay a portion of maintenance costs towards the rearing of the disabled child born of negligence and as such now have no funds left to raise an additional future healthy child.

Salih demonstrates that, were maintenance costs ever permitted as a head of damages in the future, each case must be assessed on its own facts (as opposed to a one-size-fits-all approach) so as to ensure that claimants are provided with sufficient recognition of the legal wrong they have suffered but also so as to guard against the risks of over-compensating claimants. It is however unlikely that wrongful conception cases would be treated in the same way: in these cases the intention of the claimants is quite obviously to prevent having any further children at all and so it is difficult to see how the types of restrictions on the recovery of damages in *Salih* would be capable of application to cases like *McFarlane*.

Walkin v South Manchester Health Authority: Limitation Issues

Walkin v South Manchester Health Authority[38] was a case concerning limitation. The claimant had issued a claim alleging a negligent sterilisation and claiming consequent losses. The matter came before the court on a preliminary issue as to whether the claim was statute barred. The Court of Appeal, affirming the first instance decision, held that this was a claim for damages in respect of personal injury, namely the unwanted birth, and so one limitation period (for a claim for personal injuries) applied to all heads of claim, including the harm of pregnancy and childbirth, and the financial consequences of the same.[39]

---

38 [1995] 1 WLR 1543.

39 *Ibid.* at 1555; particular focus on the judgements of Auld LJ and Neil LJ

The key points from the judgments are as follows:

- Auld LJ declined to follow Brooke J's obiter comments in *Allen v Bloomsbury*[40], a case involving negligent advice which removed the opportunity to terminate a pregnancy from the claimant. In *Allen* recovery for the pain and suffering associated with pregnancy and childbirth, as well as the financial loss arising out of the birth of the child was permitted, yet Brooke J indicated that these ought to be treated as two separate heads of loss.[41] Auld LJ rejected this suggestion, stating that it was:

  > *"… not supported by the authorities … post-natal economic loss may be unassociated with 'physical injury' in the sense that it stems from the cost of rearing a child rather than any disability in pregnancy or birth, but it is not unassociated with the cause of both, namely the unwanted pregnancy giving rise to the birth of a child."*

- Roch LJ, though ultimately agreeing with Auld LJ, expressed his own reservations, stating that he had:

  > *"… some difficulty perceiving a normal conception, pregnancy and the birth of a child as 'any disease or any impairment of a person's physical or mental condition' in cases where the only reasons for the pregnancy and subsequent birth being unwanted are financial."*[42]

- Neil LJ held that the injury occurred at the moment of conception.[43] He held that the injury was the impairment of the mother's physical condition, occasioned by the unwanted pregnancy.[44]

---

40 *Allen v Bloomsbury Health Authority* [1992] P.I.Q.R. Q50; *Ibid.*

41 *Ibid.*

42 *Walkin v South Manchester Health Authority* [1995] 1 WLR 1543 at 1555. *Ibid.*

43 *Ibid.* at 1553.

The majority decision of the Court of Appeal in *Walkin* must be correct: although maintenance costs are a financial loss they flowed from the pregnancy and childbirth, which resulted from negligence and clearly amount to an injury.[45]

The difficulty evident in the judgments in *Walkin* with accepting maintenance costs as part of a personal injury claim, alongside the differing treatment of the same issue in *Allen*, is further evidence of the struggle encountered in those cases following *Emeh*: without sufficient definition of what damages awards for maintenance costs should include, or detailed explanation as to the basis for such awards, conflicting judicial opinions and contrasting case outcomes were bound to arise.

Summary

The development of the law prior to the issue of wrongful conception and wrongful birth coming before the House of Lords in *McFarlane* is crucial to understanding the reasons why *McFarlane* was decided in the way it was.

Udale was the first wrongful conception or wrongful birth case where a claim was expressly rejected on the grounds of public policy. Early on in his judgement Jupp J highlighted the importance of ensuring that policy concerns were "*so powerful*" as to justify being applied in judicial decision making, yet he did not attempt to balance public policy with the implications a rule of non-recovery would have for claimants.[46] Ultimately however, although some of the public policy factors listed by Jupp J in *Udale* would later be denied as applicable by the House of Lords in *McFarlane*, some of his policy concerns can be seen operating in the decision making throughout the judgments of their Lordships in *McFarlane*.[47] In this way *Udale* laid the initial foundations for the argu-

44 *Ibid.* at 1555.

45 See also the later case of *Godfrey v Gloucestershire Royal Infirmary NHS Trust* [2003] EWHC 549 (Q.B.), which applies *Walkin*.

46 *Udale v Bloomsbury Area Health Authority* [1983] 1 WLR 1098 at 1103.

47 See Chapter Five.

ments against recovery for maintenance costs in wrongful conception and wrongful birth cases.

The juxtaposition of *Udale* and *Thake* illustrates the inherent subjectivity involved where there is judicial determination of public policy and highlights the associated risk of inconsistent judgments arising where public policy is the sole basis for a decision. *Emeh* did provide some temporary clarity, but it did not provide sufficient guidance on the scope or application of recovery and left subsequent courts to define the parameters.

The disordered progression of the law in the wake of *Emeh* led to *McFarlane* coming before the House of Lords. Once there, the House of Lords had to reach a judgement based on the way in which the law had been shown to develop, with no consistent reasoning demonstrated thus far. Understandably the claim brought in *McFarlane* was treated with caution by the House of Lords.

CHAPTER FIVE WRONGFUL CONCEPTION AND WRONGFUL BIRTH: MCFARLANE V TAYSIDE HEALTH BOARD

Introduction

McFarlane v Tayside Health Board is the leading authority on wrongful conception and wrongful birth cases in the UK, denying the recovery of maintenance costs in such cases.[1]

In *McFarlane* the claimants decided that they did not want to have any more children, and the husband underwent a vasectomy.[2] Unfortunately, following negligent advice as to the success of the operation, the wife became pregnant and gave birth to a healthy baby. Proceedings were then brought, claiming that the damage suffered because of the negligence included the maintenance costs of the child who had been conceived because of that negligence.[3]

In denying maintenance costs the House of Lords relied on arguments surrounding proportionality and whether extending the duty to include such losses would be fair, just and reasonable. Despite the majority denouncing public policy as a determining factor in such cases, policy concerns can be seen to operate throughout the judgments. Only Lord Millet would have awarded the claimants any sum of money to reflect the fact that they now had a child, that they had sought to avoid, to raise: he described this lump sum as a conventional award to reflect the infringement of the claimants' autonomy occasioned by the negligence.

---

1 [2000] 2 A.C. 59.

2 *Ibid.*

3 *Ibid.*

The Decisions in the Lower Courts

The case began in the Scottish courts, where the Outer House of the Court of Session denied recovery, holding that both the pain and suffering of pregnancy and the upkeep of the child were not recoverable loss.[4] Lord Gill did not recognise pregnancy as a personal injury, seeing parenthood as a 'privilege' deserved of recognition by the courts; the intrinsic benefits of parenthood always transcended any loss suffered by parents, and such loss was immeasurable in money terms regardless.[5]

On appeal in the Second Division of the Inner House of the Court of Session this decision was overturned by Lord Cullen, Lord McCluskey and Lord Allanbridge, who did not agree with the assumption that a child was a blessing for which compensation should not be awarded in every case. The court held that where negligence was proved and this had resulted in the conception of a child which the parents had sought to avoid, then that amounted to compensable damage.[6]

In particular Lord McCluskey held that it was contrary to legal principle to entitle a wrongdoer to avoid liability by requiring claimants to look to their "*prospective and impalpable gains.*" Both Lord McCluskey and Lord Cullen did not consider it appropriate for issues of public policy to be determined by the court. Lord Allanbridge accepted that there was an injury which had occurred and deemed this to have been at the moment the woman became pregnant.[7]

The House of Lords Decision

The case eventually came before the House of Lords, as the first of its type to do so. There it was held that although compensation could be awarded for the pain and suffering of pregnancy and childbirth, com-

4 *McFarlane v Tayside Health Board* 1997 S.L.T. 211 (OH).

5 *Ibid.* at 216.

6 *McFarlane v Tayside Health Board* 1998 S.C. 389 (IH).

7 *Ibid.* at 402.

pensation could not be awarded for the maintenance costs of any consequently born child.[8] Although all of their Lordships reached similar conclusions each employed different reasoning. The reasoning demonstrates a range of different concerns about the consequences of awarding maintenance costs. These included[9]:

- The difficulty in assessing quantum within appropriate bounds.
- The problem presented by offset calculations.
- The implications of awards on the value of life and on the child in question.
- The importance of properly relying on the fair, just and reasonable *Caparo* test to assess whether financial loss was recoverable in these circumstances.

Each of their Lordships' decisions warrants close examination.

Lord Slynn

Lord Slynn allowed the appeal in respect of maintenance costs, finding that these were not losses which the claimants were permitted to recover. He dismissed the appeal in respect of the other losses, so permitting recovery for the pain suffering and loss of amenity caused by the pregnancy and childbirth and expenses *"caused directly and immediately by the pregnancy and birth."*[10]

It appears that the main factor in Lord Slynn's judgment was the application of the test set out in *Caparo plc v Dickman,*[11] namely in cases concerning economic loss then alongside foreseeability of damage,

8 *McFarlane v Tayside Health Board* [2000] 2 A.C. 59 at 60.

9 *Ibid.*; *Caparo plc v Dickman* [1990] 2 A.C. 605

10 *McFarlane v Tayside Health Board* [2000] 2 A.C. 59 at 76.

11 *Caparo plc v Dickman* [1990] 2 A.C. 605.

the court must also consider whether there is a relationship of proximity and whether it would be fair, just and reasonable to impose a duty for the loss claimed. He made the following findings:

- Easily deciding in favour of the claim for damages in respect of the pregnancy and birth itself ('the mother's claim').[12]
- Holding that the liability concerned was one of economic loss, which he found to be foreseeable.[13]
- Rejecting the following arguments:
    - That public policy should or did operate in his decision making.[14]
    - That a failure to pursue abortion or adoption options constituted a break in the chain of causation, nor did it make the damage too remote (and this included any claim for maintenance costs, were they to be awarded).[15]
    - Calculating damages focussed on off-setting benefits. He found that it was too difficult a calculation unless he was prepared to assume that the benefit always outweighed the costs, which he was not.[16]
    - That it was undesirable for the child to learn that their birth was not wanted or planned. His view was that unplanned conceptions were not rare and it did not

---

12 *McFarlane v Tayside Health Board* [2000] 2 A.C. 59 at 74.

13 *Ibid.*

14 *Ibid.* at 76.

15 *Ibid.* at 74.

16 *Ibid.* at 75.

automatically follow that once the baby is born and integrated in to the family it would remain unwanted.[17]

   - That abortions would be encouraged. He considered that the ethical standards of the medical profession would be sufficient protection against this occurring.[18]

- In his view it was not however merely a matter of foreseeability or quantification of damages. He held that the central issue was as to the extent of the duty which was owed to the parent: in defining this he preferred to employ the test as set out in *Caparo*, whether there was a relationship of proximity and whether it was fair, just and reasonable for a duty to be imposed.[19]

- That whilst there was of course a duty of care to prevent pregnancy it did not automatically follow that that duty included avoiding the maintenance costs associated with any consequent child: to extend the duty that far would not be fair, just or reasonable.[20]

Lord Steyn

Lord Steyn also denied recovery of maintenance costs. He approached determination of the issue from a distributive justice standpoint: he did not find the law's usual corrective justice approach appropriate in cases such as this, involving economic loss and potential for wide-reaching liability. He did not consider it was consistent with the principles of distributive justice to allow a claim for maintenance costs.

He made the following findings:

---

17 *Ibid.*

18 *Ibid.*

19 *Ibid.* at 75 – 76; *Caparo plc v Dickman* [1990] 2 A.C. 605.

20 *McFarlane v Tayside Health Board* [2000] 2 A.C. 59 at 76.

- The claim for maintenance costs was a claim for economic loss, and the development of a new head of liability for economic loss must be justified by cogent reasons.[21]

- Conception and childbirth were capable of amounting to injuries.

- Judges ought to strive to give the real reasons behind their decisions and he did not feel that causation, foreseeability or reasonable restitution principles operated behind the denial of maintenance costs in these cases.[22]

- He rejected the following arguments[23]:

    - That there should be a set-off between the benefits and detriments of a child's life.

    - He could not conceive of any circumstances in which the decision not to resort to adoption or abortion could be questioned.[24]

- Although corrective justice would demand that parents in cases such as these be compensated for maintenance costs he preferred to approach the matter from the perspective of distributive justice, which instead demanded a focus on the distribution of burdens and losses between members of society. He accepted that this involved moral theory but asserted that the morals being applied were those of the "*commuter on the London Underground*" and not of the judges themselves: his view was that if such commuters were asked whether parents should be

---

21 *Ibid.* at 79.

22 *Ibid.* at 82.

23 *Ibid.*

24 *Ibid.* at 81.

compensated for maintenance costs the answer would be an emphatic no, based on the following considerations[25]:

- That many people are not fortunate enough to have any or any healthy children.
- That quantifying maintenance costs would entail discrimination between the rich and the poor in terms of the damages to be awarded.
- That parents would be required to argue in court that caring for their child was more trouble than it was worth.

- That in order to be consistent with *McKay v Essex Area Health Authority*[26] the parents' claim (as well as any claim brought by the child itself in a wrongful life action) did also have to be denied.[27]
- He claimed to be avoiding the "*quicksands*" of public policy in adopting this approach.[28]
- He did however also reference the unease felt by judges who have awarded maintenance costs in cases preceding *McFarlane*, citing a passage from *Jones v Berkshire Health Authority* in which Ognall J said:

  > *"... it remains a matter of surprise to me that the law acknowledges an entitlement to a mother to claim damages for the blessing of a healthy child. Certain it is that those who are afflicted with a handicapped child or who long des-*

25 *Ibid.*

26 [1982] Q.B. 1166; discussed in Chapter Three.

27 *McFarlane v Tayside Health Board* [2000] 2 A.C. 59 at 83.

28 *Ibid.*

> *perately to have a child at all and are denied that good fortune, would regard an award for this sort of contingency with a measure of astonishment."*[29]

Lord Hope of Craighead

Lord Hope of Craighead also rejected the claim for maintenance costs. His decision, like Lord Slynn, appears to have been motivated by an application of the *Caparo* test: he did not consider it to be fair, just and reasonable to include maintenance costs in the duty of care owed to the claimants. He made the following findings:

- A claim for maintenance costs is a claim for economic loss.[30]

- The law respects the right of men and women to take steps to limit the size of their family and any objection on moral or religious grounds must be rejected.[31]

- He also rejected the following arguments[32]:

    - That pregnancy and childbirth were natural processes / a normal part of life which therefore precluded them from amounting to personal injuries.

    - That any offset was necessary: he knew of no principle which required the incalculable joy following birth to be taken in to account in the assessment of damages.

- When assessing the 'mother's claim' for pain, suffering and loss of amenity, as well as financial loss, he preferred not to limit the

29 *Ibid.* at 79; *Jones v Berkshire Area Health Authority* (unreported), 2 July 1986.

30 *McFarlane v Tayside Health Board* [2000] 2 A.C. 59 at 89.

31 *Ibid.* at 86.

32 *Ibid.* at 87.

scope of recovery to the moment of birth but to apply the normal rules of remoteness when assessing the loss.[33]

- The Court of Appeal decision in *Emeh v Kensington and Chelsea and Westminster Health Authority*[34] opened the door to potentially very large damages awards and *"it might well be thought that the extent of the liability was disproportionate to the duties which were undertaken and consequently to the extent of the negligence."*[35]

- Maintenance costs were reasonably foreseeable but that was not the only criteria which needed to be satisfied when considering economic loss: a relationship of proximity and the criterion of whether imposing a duty was fair, just and reasonable, were also essential.[36]

- It was not fair, just or reasonable to leave out of account the benefits a child brings, but that as these benefits are incalculable they cannot be offset. Accordingly, he held that *"the logical conclusion as a matter of law"* was that maintenance costs were irrecoverable, being a category of economic loss which must be held to fall outside of the ambit of the duty of care owed to the claimants.[37]

- That the question of recoverability of maintenance costs was one of law and not social policy: if the law was unsatisfactory then Parliament was able to change that.[38]

---

33 *Ibid.* at 89.

34 [1985] Q.B. 1012; discussed in Chapter Four.

35 *McFarlane v Tayside Health Board* [2000] 2 A.C. 59 at 91.

36 *Ibid.* at 95.

37 *Ibid.* at 97.

38 *Ibid.*

Lord Clyde

Lord Clyde also allowed the appeal, both in denying the claim for maintenance costs and going further than the Lords before him in also excluding the claim for loss of wages and the claim for bedclothes, clothing and toiletries for a new born (the layette expenses). Lord Clyde focussed on the principles of restitution, examining what was reasonable and proportionate to include in an award of damages. He made the following findings:

- It was not an argument against recovery that quantifying a claim for maintenance costs was difficult since *"the assessment of a claim such as is presented in the present case is both practicable and practised."*[39]
- Intangible benefits could not be offset against any maintenance costs since *"like requires to be offset against like."*[40]
- There had been no break in the chain of causation by any act of the claimant, although maintenance costs were *"near the limits of the causal chain."*[41]
- The best way of approaching the question of whether maintenance costs were recoverable was to examine the ordinary principles of restitution: attempting to restore the injured party to the position they would have been in had they not suffered the wrong[42]:
    - Permitting the claimants to end up with a welcome, albeit unexpected, new addition to the family free of all cost was not just.

39 *Ibid.* at 102.

40 *Ibid.* at 103.

41 *Ibid.* at 104.

42 *Ibid.* at 104 – 106.

  - Without surrendering the child, the claimants could not be put back in to the position they would have been in but for the negligence. There was no issue of mitigation of damage however as it was not correct to suggest that the claimants ought to have availed themselves of abortion or adoption options.

  - It was not reasonable restitution to relieve the claimants of the financial obligations of caring for a child: the economic loss of maintenance costs goes far beyond any liability the defendants could reasonably have thought they were undertaking.

  - Assessing reasonableness included a consideration of proportionality: where awards including maintenance costs opened up the possibility of very large claims he could not see that there was any reasonable relationship between the fault and such a claim, such as would accord with the idea of restitution.

- Policy considerations were not a sufficiently solid ground for decision making, holding that policy considerations involved ethical or moral considerations.[43]

Lord Millet

Lord Millet allowed the appeal and dismissed all of the claims made, including the claims for pain, suffering and loss of amenity and all consequent expenses (including maintenance costs). He however felt that a conventional sum of £5,000 ought to be awarded to reflect the denial of personal autonomy that the claimants had suffered, in having lost the freedom to limit the size of their family, as a result of the defendants negligence.[44] Lord Millet's reasoning appears to be focussed on similar considerations to Lord Steyn's London Underground commuter, with

---

43 *Ibid.* at 100.

44 *Ibid.* at 114.

an examination of the way society and the law ought to view the birth of a healthy baby and a conclusion that this ought to be seen as a benefit. He made the following findings:

- The claim for maintenance costs was a claim for economic loss and such claims are tightly controlled.[45]

- An admission of a novel head of damages involves decisions on legal policy, which is distinct from public policy (though he conceded that both will involve moral considerations).[46]

- The assertion that the birth of a normal, healthy baby did not amount to harm or injury was *"not an accurate formulation of the issue."* An invasion of the claimants' legal rights incurred when the defendant failed to provide correct information and the loss occurred upon conception of an unwanted child, which represented *"an invasion of … bodily integrity and threatened further damage both physical and financial."*[47] The correct issue to focus on was whether the particular heads of damage being claimed were recoverable as a matter of law.[48]

- In principle any losses occasioned by pregnancy and birth are the very things which the defendant was meant to prevent and are recoverable regardless of how they are categorised. He was not persuaded that the remedy sought was disproportionate to the wrong.[49]

45 *Ibid.* at 109.

46 *Ibid.* at 108.

47 *Ibid.* at 107.

48 *Ibid.* at 108.

49 *Ibid.* at 109.

- However, he still found that there was *"something distasteful, if not morally offensive, in treating the birth of a normal, healthy child as a matter for compensation."*[50]

- The parents' motivation in undertaking the operation was not a relevant consideration to recovery of damages.[51]

- He was not convinced that offsetting the benefits provided by a child against the financial cost was a realistic or practical way of dealing with recovery.[52]

- He accepted the main thrust of the two principal arguments behind previous dismissals of claims for maintenance costs, which he held to be:

    i. That a healthy baby was a blessing: when discussing the benefits and detriments of a child he held that parents were entitled to *"decide for themselves where their own interests lie. But society itself must regard the balance as beneficial."* He was of the view that where the law regarded an event as beneficial then claimants could not *"make it a matter for compensation merely by saying that it is an event they did not want to happen."*[53]

    ii. That such costs have been occasioned by the parents' deliberate decision to keep the child. He did however view it as repugnant to suggest that it was unreasonable for parents to decide against abortion or adoption and he did not consider that such a choice broke the chain of causation.[54]

---

50 *Ibid.* at 111.

51 *Ibid.* at 110.

52 *Ibid.* at 111.

53 Ibid. at 110 and 112.

54 *Ibid.* at 110 and 113 – 114.

- In an analysis much like Lord Steyn's London Underground commuter he was of the view that, in an instinctive reaction people may have difficulty articulating the reasoning behind:

> *"... it would be generally regarded as unacceptable (and probably unethical) for a surgeon to seek by contract to limit the damages for which he might be liable for his professional negligence. But I suspect that most people would regard it as reasonable for a surgeon who performed a sterilisation to attempt to exclude liability for the costs of bringing up a child whose birth he negligently failed to prevent."*[55]

The majority decision of the House of Lords was therefore to allow the claim for pain, suffering and loss of amenity and immediate financial costs occasioned by pregnancy and childbirth, but to deny the claim for maintenance costs.

Summary

As can be seen, the focus of the majority in *McFarlane* was on whether an award which included maintenance costs would be fair, just and reasonable, and whether such an award would be proportionate to the liability taken on by clinicians.

Under normal tortious principles where there is proven negligence, no break in the chain of causation and damage which is not too remote (such that it was within the reasonable contemplation of the clinician), recovery would follow. It is difficult to reconcile a finding that the inclusion of maintenance costs would not be fair, just or reasonable with the fact that the medical procedures which are the subject of such claims are undertaken for the sole purpose of avoiding further children, and the financial cost of rearing a child is the ordinary consequence of a child being born to these parents.

---

55 *Ibid.* at 109.

Examining proportionality is also a departure from the usual application of tortious principles: it is not normally the case that simply because the consequences of a negligent act are far reaching and represent a significant financial loss the defendant is permitted to escape liability for that loss.

Nonetheless these were the reasons given by their Lordships in denying recovery. The majority of their Lordships also expressly stated that policy was not operating in their decision making. It does however at times appear that policy concerns influenced the reasoning of their Lordships. One example can be found in the judgment of Lord Steyn who, although explicitly stating that his decision was not based on public policy, also cited Ognall J expressing surprise in a previous case that the law permitted compensation for the "blessing" of a child. That this appears in Lord Steyn's judgment at all is suggestive that the belief that a healthy child is a blessing (an obvious public policy factor, acknowledged as such in previous cases) did operate in his own decision making. Lord Hope and Lord Clyde's judgments also included discussion of the benefits and joy a child brings, and again appeared to be focussed on the idea of a child as a blessing. Such discussions do not properly engage with the fact that the claimants in wrongful conception and wrongful birth cases took steps to avoid having that further child, regardless of the value which society or the courts place on that life.

There is also much discussion surrounding offset calculations, weighing the benefits and detriments of a child against one another. As is recognised by some of their Lordships this balancing exercise is usually only applied when the benefits and detriments are commensurate (i.e. both financial, as opposed to weighing intangible benefits against financial detriments). Interestingly, it is only Lord Millet (and not even in the context of discussing offset calculations) who confronts the existence of an intangible detriment to the parents, of having had their personal autonomy infringed through the frustration of their previous reproductive choice (i.e. the negligence having prevented them from exercising their right not to conceive any more children). This illustrates the myriad of considerations involved with, and the difficulty in entering into, offset calculations.

The discussion of the value of life throughout the judgments risks mixing up moral argument with legal principle, focussing on the way in which such litigation might impact on the life of a child or our perception of the value of life instead of looking at the legal wrong which has been suffered and the consequences of the same.

Lord Steyn uses his London Underground commuter as a way to justify the denial of maintenance costs. There is however an inherent risk of subjectivity when relying on distributive justice in wrongful conception and wrongful birth cases. This ordinary man construct is subjective by its very nature. In using it what is really happening is an imputation of Lord Steyn's own opinion to a fictional independent observer on the Underground.[56] The difficulty with subjective tests such as this can be seen in the differing views presented by their Lordships throughout *McFarlane* itself. Certainly, Lord Millet appears not to be in accord with the rest of their Lordships as to the demands of distributive justice, awarding the conventional sum of damages so as to ensure that the parents were not, as he puts it, left empty-handed.

Additionally, aside from Lord Millet the judgements in *McFarlane* appear to focus solely on the financial impact on the clinician, with little regard to the impact a rule denying recovery will have on the claimants, who will then be left to shoulder the financial burden of raising a child (a burden they had actively sought to avoid through undertaking the medical procedure which is now the subject of a negligence action). It was open to their Lordships to forge an exception to the normal rules of recovery, creating limits to keep the award in line with the *Caparo* test or the principles of distributive justice, without denying recovery outright. It does not however appear that such a middle-ground was entertained by any of their Lordships other than Lord Millet.

It is obvious that the House of Lords were concerned about opening the floodgates to potentially far reaching claims for maintenance costs.

56 See the judgment of Hale LJ in *Parkinson v St James and Seacroft University Hospital NHS Trust* [2001] EWCA Civ 530, discussed more fully in Chapter Six.

Whilst it is important to recognise the legal wrong suffered by claimants and ensure proper compensation it is also important to retain limits on recovery. There is however no discussion in the judgments in *McFarlane* of an alternative way of striking this balance (such as imposing a financial cap on recovery for example), with their Lordships instead opting for a blanket denial of maintenance costs.

The judgments in McFarlane presented a mix of different reasoning, from which subsequent courts had to select the best way to deal with cases which presented factual variations to *McFarlane*. The House of Lords dealt only with the case of a healthy baby and did not provide guidance on whether the principles set down in relation to maintenance costs would apply to all children regardless of health. The question of maintenance costs in wrongful conception and wrongful birth claims was therefore to come before the courts again.[57]

57 Discussed in Chapters Six and Seven.

CHAPTER SIX WRONGFUL CONCEPTION AND WRONGFUL BIRTH: MCFARLANE RE-VISITED IN PARKINSON V ST JAMES AND SEACROFT UNIVERSITY HOSPITAL NHS TRUST

Introduction

Following *McFarlane* it wasn't long before the court was once again asked to examine the issue of the recoverability of maintenance costs in wrongful conception and wrongful birth claims. Despite a recognition within the judgments in *McFarlane* that there may well be factual variations which would alter the outcome, their Lordships made only passing reference to what those factual variations would be, and so made no determination on the question of a child who was not healthy. As such their Lordships left the question of recoverability of damages in cases where the child was born with a disability open.

The lack of any determination by the House of Lords on what would happen were a disabled baby born in a wrongful conception case led to the Court of Appeal re-examining the question of maintenance costs in *Parkinson v St James and Seacroft University Hospital NHS Trust*.[1] *Parkinson* concerned a claim where a disabled baby had been born following an allegedly negligent sterilisation operation, but where the disability was not itself a product of that negligence. The claimant sought damages for the unwanted pregnancy and childbirth, including maintenance costs for the child.

In *Parkinson* it was held that a claim for the extra maintenance costs associated with the child's disability should succeed. Brooke LJ applied the *Caparo* test to the facts in *Parkinson* and found that it was fair, just

1 [2001] EWCA Civ 530; [2002] Q.B. 266.

and reasonable to allow an award of damages relating to the maintenance costs occasioned by the disability of the child. Hale LJ was critical of the reasoning in *McFarlane* and did not consider it appropriate to extend what she described as the *"limitation on the damages which would otherwise be recoverable on normal principles"* created by *McFarlane*. Accordingly, she held that the extra maintenance costs related to the child's disability ought to be awarded.

The Decision of the Court of Appeal

The claim first came before Longmore J on a preliminary issue as to the recoverability of damages. He held that the claimant could not recover for the child's basic maintenance costs but that she should be able to recover for the additional costs of providing for her child's *"special needs and care"* which were occasioned by virtue of the disability.[2]

The Court of Appeal affirmed the first instance judgement, holding that the extra maintenance costs associated with the disability were recoverable as the conception and birth of a disabled child was a reasonably foreseeable consequence of the negligence.[3] It was also held that what constituted a significant disability would have to be decided on a case-by-case basis.

Brooke LJ delivered the lead judgment. He found the 'special upbringing' costs associated with disability to be recoverable. He found that limiting the award to those additional costs satisfied the tests of foreseeability, proximity and was also fair, just and reasonable.

Hale LJ also delivered a lengthy judgment. She was of the view that *McFarlane* resulted in a limitation on the damages which would ordinarily be recoverable under normal tortious principles and she was not content to extend that limitation any further. She therefore found the extra costs associated with disability to be recoverable. She also strongly

2 *Parkinson v St James and Seacroft University Hospital NHS Trust* [2002] Q.B. 266 at 270.

3 *Ibid.* at 283.

emphasised the profound impact the negligence in these cases has on the lives of the parents, particularly of the mother.

Sir Martin Nourse was in agreement with the judgments of Brooke LJ and Hale LJ Accordingly the appeals were dismissed, and the Court of Appeal set down a new rule of recovery in wrongful conception and wrongful birth claims: if the child conceived or born of negligence was also born with a disability then claimants would be able to recover for the additional maintenance costs associated with the disability.

Brooke LJ

Brooke LJ felt that the law had moved on since the early wrongful conception and wrongful birth cases pre-dating *McFarlane* and held that their Lordships in *McFarlane* had left open the issue of recoverability where the child born of negligence was disabled. In his view it was in accordance with the test set out by their Lordships in *McFarlane* to permit recovery of the extra maintenance costs associated with the child's disability.

The key parts of his judgement are as follows:

- He held that the law of negligence was more complicated than it was when *Emeh v Kensington and Westminster and Chelsea Health Authority*[4] was decided: at the time that *Parkinson* came before the Court of Appeal there were a number of different techniques available when determining liability and there was *"no longer a single 'correct' test."*[5]

4 [1985] Q.B. 1012; see Chapter Four for a full discussion of this case and other cases preceding *McFarlane* and *Parkinson*.

5 *Parkinson v St James and Seacroft University Hospital NHS Trust* [2002] Q.B. 266 at 273 and 276.

- He highlighted two factors which had recently emerged when assessing liability[6]:

    i. That courts should examine the purpose for which the service was rendered when defining the limits of the duty owed.

    ii. That distributive justice may be deployed to assist the court in difficult cases.

- Having considered the judgments in *McFarlane* he found that their Lordships were agreed on the following[7]:

    - That public policy played no part in the decision-making process, though this was distinct from legal policy.

    - That the birth of a child was the foreseeable consequence of a negligently performed sterilisation operation.

    - The parents' claim was a claim for economic loss.

    - The fact that the parents had declined to exercise their right to have an abortion or pursue adoption options did not operate to reduce or reject their claim.

    - That the 'benefits rule' employed in other jurisdictions (where the benefits of a child were offset against the financial burden of a child) did not present a solution in wrongful conception and wrongful birth claims.

6 *Ibid.* at 274.

7 *Ibid.* at 277 – 278.

- Insofar as there was no dissenting voice presented on these issues, there was also passive agreement that the claim should not be refused because of:

  i. Concerns that this would lead doctors to encourage late abortions or;

  ii. The effect on a child of learning that they were not wanted.

- His analysis of the decision of the House of Lords in *McFarlane* was that the majority (Lords Hope, Slynn and Steyn) had asked whether the particular facts of *McFarlane* justified the law recognising an enforceable duty of care to parents to relieve them of the financial consequence of child rearing[8]:

  - Lord Slynn had examined proximity, the *Caparo* test (whether the duty in question was fair, just and reasonable) and whether there had been an assumption of responsibility. As these tests had been applied to the facts of *McFarlane* only briefly it was not clear whether Lord Slynn would have applied these tests in the same way were the child disabled.

  - The judgments of Lord Hope and Steyn demonstrated that the application of the *Caparo* test was inexorably linked to the concept of distributive justice.

  - Lord Steyn expressly stated that the outcome might be different were the child born of negligence also born handicapped.

- He did not find previous authority concerning wrongful birth claims where the child was born disabled helpful. There were a series of first instance judgments in which it had been held, at

8 *Ibid.* at 278.

first instance, that *McFarlane* did not preclude an award of damages:

- *Rand v East Dorset Health Authority*: Newman J was concerned with a Down's syndrome child.[9]

- *Hardman v Amin*: Henriques K. was concerned with a child who was born severely disabled after his mother contracted rubella during her pregnancy.[10]

- *Lee v Taunton and Somerset NHS Trust*: Toulson J was concerned with a child born with a large spina bifida lesion and hydrocephalus.[11]

He considered that the policy issues in such cases were different and so did not assist in the determination of the facts in *Parkinson* itself, which was a wrongful conception case.[12]

- He permitted recovery of the additional maintenance costs associated with disability on the following basis[13]:

  - The birth of a child with congenital disabilities was reasonably foreseeable.

  - The potential claimants were limited in number, being just Mrs Parkinson who had been subject to the operation and any sexual partner she may have.

9 [2000] Lloyd's Med Rep 181.

10 [2000] Lloyd's Med Rep 498.

11 [2001] FLR 419.

12 *Parkinson v St James and Seacroft University Hospital NHS Trust* [2002] Q.B. 266 at 282.

13 *Ibid.* at 282 – 283.

  - There was no difficulty in principle in deeming the surgeon to have assumed responsibility for the *"foreseeable and disastrous economic consequences of performing his services negligently."*

  - The purpose of the operation was to prevent the conception of any further children, including children with congenital disabilities, and the duty of care owed was strictly related to the proper fulfilment of that purpose.

  - It was not a radical step into the unknown to permit recovery since parents in such cases had been entitled to recover damages for 15 years between the decision in *Emeh* and the issue coming before the House of Lords in *McFarlane*.

  - The tests of foreseeability and proximity were therefore satisfied, and it was fair, just and reasonable to permit an award limited to the 'special costs of upbringing' associated with the child's disability.

- He acknowledged that there should be no liability where the disabilities were brought about by an intervening cause between conception and birth and also held that what constituted a significant disability for the purposes of this type of award would have to be decided on a case-by-case basis.[14]

Hale LJ

Hale LJ, as she then was, also delivered judgment. She was the first female judge to provide insight into this issue, an issue which was central to women's rights, and so her judgment is arguably the most important and warrants particular attention.

---

14 *Ibid.* at 283.

She began her judgment with the powerful statement that *"the right to bodily integrity is the first and most important of the interests protected by the law of tort."* She held that this right comprised[15]:

i. The right to physical autonomy: making one's own autonomous choices about what happens to one's body.

ii. The right not to be subjected to any injury or harm.

She held that economic interests fell as a much lower consideration than the right to bodily integrity and that somewhere in the middle fell those cases where the invasion of this right to bodily integrity had itself caused financial loss to a claimant.[16]

On an analysis of the judgments in *McFarlane* Hale LJ held that all of their Lordships had recognised the affront to bodily integrity, though each in their own different ways, and held that pregnancy and childbirth were *"none the less an invasion because they are the result of natural processes."*[17] She held that in wrongful conception and wrongful birth cases there were serious consequences for both mothers and fathers but emphasised that there were *"undoubted and inescapable differences between the sexes."*[18] In discussing the impact that pregnancy and childbirth has on a woman Hale LJ made the following observations[19]:

- There are profound physical and psychological changes associated with pregnancy and childbirth.

- That sometimes pregnancy and childbirth are difficult and dangerous for women.

15 *Ibid.* at 284.

16 *Ibid.*

17 *Ibid.* at 285.

18 *Ibid.*

19 *Ibid.* at 285 – 286.

- Continuing with pregnancy brings a host of lesser infringements on personal autonomy, for example not being able to wear your favourite clothes or having to change your diet.

- Labour itself, aptly named, is hard work and dangerous.

- Personal autonomy is curtailed far further than simply pregnancy and childbirth since *"literally, one's life is no longer just one's own but also someone else's. One cannot simply rid oneself of that responsibility."*

- *"The invasion of the mother's personal autonomy does not stop once her body and mind have returned to their pre-pregnancy state"* since the mother will always be the legal mother, with all of the legal and parental responsibilities and potential criminal liability which attaches to parenthood.

- She emphasised that parental responsibility was more than just financial responsibility and that much like the labour involved in childbirth the bringing up of a child was hard work.

Bound by the House of Lords in *McFarlane* Hale LJ was not able to depart from the principles set out therein in denying the recovery of maintenance costs for a healthy child. She, like Brooke LJ, felt that the recovery of the additional maintenance costs associated with disability ought to be permitted in *Parkinson*. She found that the issue of such recoverability had been left open by their Lordships in *McFarlane* and she was not prepared to extend the limitations imposed by *McFarlane* any further.[20]

She made the following findings:

- That the law already recognises claims for care and assistance where this is provided by family or friends of an injured person [21]:

---

20 *Ibid.* at 293.

- Such a claim is made by the injured person even though the loss is properly that of the family or friends (who themselves have not suffered any injury or wrong).

- In wrongful conception and wrongful birth claims the care is provided by the very person who has suffered the wrong and so *"the legal obligation to provide it is the direct and foreseeable consequence of that wrong."*

- She expressed surprise that there had been no analysis of wrongful conception and wrongful birth claims in this way: in fact, no claim had ever been brought for the care provided and focus had been instead on all of the financial expenditure associated with child rearing, such costs being part and parcel of the very same caring responsibility (not separate from it).

- The mother's financial claim represented *"the consequences of the fundamental invasion of her rights, which was the conception itself"* and she did not therefore feel it was possible to draw a 'clean line' under the losses at birth.[22]

- She held that, as had been recognised by a majority of their Lordships in *McFarlane*, *"on normal principles of tortious liability, once it was established that the pregnancy had been wrongfully caused, compensation would be payable for all those consequences, whether physical or financial, which are capable of sounding in damages."* She asserted that the object of the service which had been provided to the claimant was to prevent pregnancy and the surgeon was under a duty of care to perform that service with reasonable care and skill. [23]

---

21 *Ibid.* at 287.

22 *Ibid.*

23 *Ibid.* at 288.

- She acknowledged that notwithstanding the above all of their Lordships rejected the claim for maintenance costs in *McFarlane* and did so with differing reasoning. She re-iterated that the decision in *McFarlane* was binding authority but described it as *"a limitation on the damages which would otherwise be recoverable on normal principles."*[24] On an analysis of the judgments she was of the view that[25]:

  - The majority of their Lordships accepted that there was the existence of some duty and then went on to consider whether a particular type of damage would be recoverable were that duty to be broken.

  - At the heart of their Lordships' answer to the above question there was *"a feeling that to compensate for the financial costs of bringing up a healthy child is a step too far"* and that since a child brought benefits as well as costs the only sensible course was to assume that these cancelled each other out (describing this as the 'deemed equilibrium' solution reached by their Lordships).[26]

  - That many would challenge the assumption that the benefits of a child cancelled out the cost and in any event she did not agree with the commodification of a child which occurred when one regarded the child as an asset to the parents.

  - She was also not convinced by the 'deemed equilibrium' solution, holding that were it true that a child was an asset then the law could have simply assigned that benefit a sum of money, which itself could then have been deducted from the overall costs.

24 *Ibid.* at 293.

25 *Ibid.* at 289 – 292.

26 *Ibid.* at 292 – 293.

- Lord Slynn's conclusion that it was not fair, just and reasonable to extend the duty to permit recovery of maintenance costs since the doctor had not assumed responsibility for such losses was difficult to follow since *"the doctor clearly does assume responsibility for preventing conception"* and the losses resulting from conception and claimed for were *"clearly foreseeable, indeed highly probable"*.

- Lord Steyn's London Underground commuter would not present a representative sample of public opinion and was really *"being invoked not as a hypothetical reasonable man but as a moral arbiter."* She did not believe that the response of the public would be as emphatic and unanimous as the London Underground commuter example made out it would be, pointing to the fact that so many judges all over the world had reached different conclusions on the same issue.

- She re-asserted Lord Millet's view that the benefits of a child to society and to an individual were two different things.

- That distributive justice was concerned with fairness not just between different classes of defendant and claimant but also between different classes of potential claimant (i.e. those who give birth to a healthy child versus those who give birth to a disabled child), and so it was not inconsistent with distributive justice principles to permit recovery where the potential claimant conceived a disabled child.[27]

- That there was a sufficient relationship of proximity with the mother in these claims, whether or not she was the subject of the operation herself.[28]

---

27 *Ibid.* at 290.

28 *Ibid.* at 294.

- That a disabled child required *"extra care and extra expenditure"* and that this was all the award of maintenance costs reflected, it did not alter the dignity or status of a disabled child who should be treated as having the exact same worth as a healthy child.[29]

- As to how to determine whether disability was sufficient to permit recovery:

    - She pointed to legislation which already provided a definition of disability, such as the *Children Act 1989*, and suggested using those same definitions.[30]

    - She preferred to use birth as the cut off for the point by which the disability must have arisen.[31]

Hale LJ also discussed the consequences for fathers in such cases. She was of the view that there were two types of harm in wrongful conception and wrongful birth cases: a harm to bodily integrity and an obligation to care for and bring up a child. It was only the latter of these which was suffered by the father. However, she considered that if there was a sufficient relationship of proximity between the tortfeasor and the father then he would also have a claim.[32]

Summary

McFarlane only implicitly acknowledged that there would be factual variations affecting the outcome for claimants. The first factual variation came in the form of *Parkinson* and the birth of a disabled child following an allegedly negligent sterilisation, but where the disability itself had not been caused by that negligence. The Court of Appeal in

29 *Ibid.* 293.

30 *Ibid.* at 293 – 294.

31 *Ibid.* at 294, see her detailed reasons for so finding set out at [92].

32 See Chapter Nine for further discussion on a father's rights in these claims.

Parkinson was in a difficult position: they had to reach a decision by building upon the reasoning of their Lordships in *McFarlane*, being a lower court bound by the decision of the House of Lords, without the House of Lords having provided guidance on the way to approach claims involving disabled children. This task was made even more difficult as all of the judgments in *McFarlane* presented different viewpoints: Brooke LJ himself describing their Lordships as having spoken *"with five different voices."*[33]

Although both Lord Clyde and Lord Steyn made reference to disability as a distinguishing factor in *McFarlane* they did not go further to explain how disability excluded such cases from the reach of their decisions.[34] Further, all of the tests used as the basis of the decision to deny recovery in *McFarlane* become even more acute where a clinician is being asked to compensate for the costs of a disability which he did not himself cause. Arguments against recovery based on the *Caparo* test, distributive justice or proportionality loom larger in the case of a disabled child given the extra costs associated with that disability. Basing recovery on disability also exacerbates issues regarding the value of life as it suggests that the fact of the child's disability has changed the perception that life is not ordinarily something for which compensation should be provided and as such risks categorising the lives of those who suffer from a disability as having lower social value.

It is therefore difficult to see the outcome of *Parkinson* as consistent with *McFarlane* and at times it appears to be a direct challenge to *McFarlane* instead, with much of what Brooke LJ says about foreseeability being equally applicable to healthy children and with Hale LJ expressly stating her disagreement with some of the reasoning in *McFarlane*. Nonetheless neither Brooke LJ nor Hale LJ explicitly acknowledge that there is any inconsistency between their own findings and those of the House of Lords in *McFarlane*: Hale LJ simply stating that she does not consider it appropriate to extend the limitations of

33 *Parkinson v St James and Seacroft University Hospital NHS Trust* [2002] Q.B. 266 at 277.

34 See Chapter Five for further detailed discussion on the judgments in *McFarlane v Tayside Health Board* [2000] 2 A.C. 59.

McFarlane further and Brooke LJ relying on the same tests of foreseeability, proximity and whether it is fair, just and reasonable to extend the duty (the exact same tests used in *McFarlane*) to permit the recovery of additional costs.

There still remained unanswered questions following *Parkinson*: Brooke LJ's obiter comments that there were different policy considerations at play in wrongful birth claims casts uncertainty over the extent to which the outcome in *Parkinson* would be the same in a wrongful birth, as opposed to wrongful conception, action. *Parkinson* also left subsequent courts to determine on a case-by-case basis whether a child was sufficiently disabled to be awarded maintenance costs, and whether there was a sufficient causal link between the birth and disability.

The later case of *Groom v Selby* (with Brooke LJ and Hale LJ again delivering judgment) does respond to some of these unanswered questions.[35] In that case a child was born when the claimant's GP failed to identify that the claimant was pregnant at the time of a sterilisation and so deprived the claimant of the opportunity to terminate the pregnancy: the claim was therefore one for wrongful birth. The child was born prematurely and four weeks later developed salmonella meningitis as a result of which she became severely handicapped. The Court of Appeal held that the claimant was entitled to claim damages for wrongful birth, to include a claim for the extra maintenance costs associated with the child's disability. It was held that the child was not a 'healthy child' at birth since the bacterium responsible for the meningitis was already present on her skin and there had therefore been no novus actus interveniens. It was also held that the birth of a premature child, who developed salmonella meningitis as a result of her exposure to bacterium during the normal birth process, was a foreseeable consequence of the defendant's negligence. Accordingly, the claimant was awarded damages for the extra maintenance costs associated with her child's disability. This case does provide insight in to the way in which disability and causation will be assessed by the courts but of course does not provide a complete picture, since again the Court of Appeal did not provide any defined limits to guide subsequent courts (which was something Brooke

35 [2001] EWCA Civ 1522.

LJ himself acknowledged in *Groom*[36]). Although *Groom* does at least appear to provide Court of Appeal authority for treating wrongful birth and wrongful conception cases the same, it should be noted that Brooke LJ's judgment does not expressly state this (though Hale LJ's does) and he appears to distinguish between wrongful birth cases like *Groom v Selby*, where there was no possibility of detecting the presence of a disability by foetal testing, and those where it was.[37]

Parkinson also dealt only with the situation where a child was disabled but did not address or appear to even consider what the outcome would be were one of the parents disabled. *Parkinson* was not the end of the development of the law surrounding wrongful conception and wrongful birth claims, with *Rees v Darlington Memorial Hospital NHS Trust*[38] presenting yet another factual variation on *McFarlane* and addressing the issue of disabled parents. *Rees* is examined in Chapter Seven.

36 *Ibid.* at [26].

37 *Ibid.* at [19]; see also obiter comment on this issue in *Rees v Darlington Memorial Hospital NHS Trust* [2004] 1 A.C. 309, discussed in full in Chapter Seven; see also *Meadows v Khan* [2017] EWHC (Q.B.), discussed in full in Chapter Nine.

38 [2004] 1 A.C. 309.

CHAPTER SEVEN WRONGFUL CONCEPTION AND WRONGFUL BIRTH: MCFARLANE RE-VISITED (AGAIN) IN REES V DARLINGTON MEMORIAL HOSPITAL NHS TRUST

Introduction

Rees v Darlington Memorial Hospital NHS Trust[1] presented another factual variation to *McFarlane*. This time a claim was brought by a mother who was herself seriously disabled and who had elected to have a sterilisation operation because of the difficulties she would face in raising children with her disability. The sterilisation was performed negligently, which resulted in the conception of a healthy baby. She then brought a claim for maintenance costs, which included the extra costs associated with her own disability.

It fell to the House of Lords to determine whether *Rees* presented an extension of *Parkinson v St James and Seacroft University Hospital NHS Trust*,[2] in that the disability of the mother altered the circumstances so as to allow recovery for additional maintenance costs, or a straight forward application of *McFarlane*, being a case concerning a healthy child and thereby falling outside of recovery.

In *Rees* it was held by a narrow majority that the disability of the parent did not alter the application of *McFarlane* and that accordingly any claim for maintenance costs should fail. The minority judgments however considered disability to be a distinguishing factor and would have permitted an award of damages to reflect the extra maintenance costs occasioned by such disability. Despite denying the claim in *Rees* the majority in the House of Lords did still modify the principles set

---

1 [2004] 1 A.C. 309.

2 [2001] EWCA Civ 530; discussed in Chapter Six.

down by *McFarlane* through the creation of a conventional award of £15,000, to reflect the legal wrong suffered by the claimant in these cases.

The Journey to the House of Lords

At first instance, the case coming before the court on a preliminary issue as to recoverability of damages, Mr Stuart Brown QC held that the claimant was not entitled to recover for the maintenance costs she was seeking.[3]

The claimant appealed that decision, which a majority of the Court of Appeal allowed in part (Hale LJ and Robert LJJ allowing the appeal in part and Waller LJ dissenting). The majority held that it was fair, just and reasonable to award any 'extra' maintenance costs which were *"attributable to and incurred as a result of the fact of the parent's disability"* and that, as the facts in *Rees* were not covered by *McFarlane*, such a decision was a legitimate extension to *Parkinson*.[4]

The case then came before the House of Lords, with seven Law Lords presiding. A majority of the House of Lords allowed the defendant's appeal and held that recovery for maintenance costs should be denied in *Rees* as the facts were more in line with *McFarlane* than *Parkinson*. A 'conventional award' was however permitted to reflect the legal wrong that had been done to Ms Rees through the negligence of the clinician.[5]

The majority of the House of Lords considered that there was no reason to depart from the decision in *McFarlane* and based their decision on the following:

---

3 *Rees v Darlington Memorial Hospital NHS Trust* [2004] 1 A.C. 309 at 309, 320 and 341.

4 *Ibid.*

5 *Ibid.* at 309.

- That considerations of what was fair, just and reasonable and the demands of distributive justice precluded any such award.
- Concerns regarding the impossibility of quantifying the benefits of parenthood.
- That it was inappropriate to regard a child as solely a financial liability.

As in *McFarlane*, their Lordships did not speak with one voice and the decision in *Rees* was by a majority of only four, each of whom presented different viewpoints, with Lord Steyn, Lord Hope of Craighead and Lord Hutton dissenting. As such once again each of the judgments warrants close examination.

Lord Bingham of Cornhill and Lord Nicholls of Birkenhead

Lord Bingham of Cornhill and Lord Nicholls of Birkenhead delivered similar judgments, and both appeared to base their decisions on principles of distributive justice, re-iterating some of the policy considerations set out in *McFarlane*. Subject to one 'gloss' (awarding a 'conventional award' of £15,000 to reflect the legal wrong suffered), they adhered to and affirmed the decision in *McFarlane* in rejecting the claim for maintenance costs.[6]

Lord Bingham of Cornhill

Lord Bingham of Cornhill made the following findings:

- That all of their Lordships in *McFarlane* gave different reasons for denying recovery but that it seemed to him that all were moved by reasons of legal, as opposed to public, policy. The policy considerations were as follows[7]:

6 *Ibid.* at 314 and 316.

7 *Ibid.* at 315 and 316.

- An unwillingness to regard even an unwanted child as a *"financial liability and nothing else."*

- A recognition of the difficulty in quantifying the potential rewards of parenthood.

- That awarding *"potentially very large sums of damages to parents of a normal and healthy child against a National Health Service always in need of funds to meet pressing demands would rightly offend the community's sense of how public resources should be allocated."*

- That a full award of damages towards maintenance costs (subject to the ordinary limits of foreseeability and remoteness) with no discount for any benefits was what *"an orthodox application of familiar and conventional principles of the law of tort would … have pointed towards"*, leaving Parliament to enact any limitations on that award.[8]

- Notwithstanding the above it would not be appropriate to disturb the decision in *McFarlane*, which was delivered only 4 years prior, and he was not persuaded that arguments which had been rejected then should be accepted in this case or that the policy considerations at play then had lost their potency.[9]

- It was a concern that the parents in such claims were victims of a legal wrong who would be denied any recompense, other than an award immediately relating to the pregnancy and childbirth. He therefore supported the idea of a 'conventional award' put forward by Lord Millett in *McFarlane*, which he set at the sum of £15,000 and which would be awarded to all parents regardless of whether they or the child had a disability. The conventional award was not intended to be compensatory or the product of any calculation, but it would simply "… *afford some*

8 *Ibid.* at 314.

9 *Ibid.* at 316.

measure of recognition of the wrong done. And it would afford a more ample measure of justice than the pure McFarlane rule."[10]

- Criticising the decision in *Parkinson* as follows[11]:
  - That it resulted in the extent of the defendant's liability depending on a disability which the doctor's negligence did not cause, rather than on the birth which it did cause.
  - It was undesirable that parents would be encouraged to portray themselves or their child as disabled in order to recover damages.
  - It was difficult to quantify the additional costs attributable to a disability in a state where there was provision of social care.

Lord Nicholls of Birkenhead

Lord Nicholls of Birkenhead made the following findings:

- The law's evaluation of damages was not always a mechanical exercise and recovery of damages depended on considerations of fairness and reasonableness. Those were questions for the courts to determine; in doing so judges did not have any special insight in to what contemporary society regarded as fair, just and reasonable but ought to still form a view even in difficult or controversial cases.[12]
- *McFarlane* determined that fairness and reasonableness did not require that recoverable damages should extend as far as main-

---

10 *Ibid.* at 317.

11 *Ibid.*

12 *Ibid.* at 318.

tenance costs and he had not heard anything in *Rees* to persuade him otherwise[13]:

- It would be a disproportionate response to the wrong to require a doctor or the NHS to pay all of the costs of bringing up a child.

- Recovery did not accord with the value society attaches to human life and parenthood.

- The birth of a child should not be treated as akin to personal injury.

- It was fair, just and reasonable to award a conventional sum in recognition that a legal wrong had been suffered which has a far-reaching effect on the lives of the parents.[14]

Lord Millet

Lord Millet was one of the Law Lords sitting in *McFarlane*. In *McFarlane* he provided a dissent as he would have allowed a 'conventional award' (like that now awarded in *Rees*) and his judgment in *Rees* is thus of particular interest. In his judgment in *Rees* he made clear that in *McFarlane* the issue of a disabled child had been left open precisely because it was felt that that might be a distinguishable set of facts and, although he wished to leave the issue open, he would be prepared to award the extra maintenance costs associated with a child's disability. He did not however consider that this exception ought to extend to disabled parents and he still regarded the proper outcome in *Rees* to be a denial of the claim for maintenance costs, but with an award of a conventional sum instead. He appeared to base his reasoning on principles of distributive justice, focussing again on his views of the benefits which a healthy child brings (even to a disabled parent).

---

13 *Ibid.* at 318 and 319.

14 *Ibid.* at 319.

He made the following findings:

- *McFarlane* should not be overturned, even if on further reflection he thought he had decided incorrectly, since the criteria for the House of Lords overturning one of its own decisions were *"nowhere near satisfied."* He was in any event satisfied that *McFarlane* had been decided correctly.[15]

- He clarified the basis of his decision in *McFarlane* as follows[16]:

    - There was no difficulty with causation, whether factual or legal as *"the pregnancy and birth of a child are the very things which the defendants are employed to prevent"* and *"it is impossible to say that consequential loss falls outside the scope of their duty of care."*

    - The *"novelty of the claim in McFarlane lay in one particular head of damage – the cost of bringing up a healthy child,"* which the House of Lords considered it would be morally repugnant to award damages for.

    - Hale LJ's analysis of a 'deemed equilibrium' was not correct and that none of the speeches had adopted this approach.[17]

- Further clarifying the basis on which *McFarlane* had been decided he stated that:

    "The conventional approach to damages would allow the costs of bringing up a healthy child, but only so far as they were reasonable. Costs which are incurred unreasonably are not recoverable. So what McFarlane decides is that the costs

---

15 *Ibid.* at 343.

16 *Ibid.* at 345 – 346.

17 See discussion of Hale LJ's judgment in *Parkinson* above.

> *of bringing up a healthy child, even though reasonably incurred, are not recoverable.*
>
> ...
>
> *In principle, the same must be true of the disabled parent. To the extent that her disability has any effect, it increases the amount of costs which she reasonably incurs in bringing up the child, costs which are nevertheless not recoverable."*[18]

- It wasn't necessary to decide whether *Parkinson* had been correctly decided and he preferred to keep the issue open. He did however confirm that *McFarlane* was expressly confined to *"the case of a healthy child because we recognised that the case of a disabled child might be distinguishable."* He was of the view that *"a disabled child is not 'worth' less than a healthy one. The blessings of his or her birth are no less incalculable. Society must equally 'regard the balance as beneficial'."* However, he also considered that there would be a difference in the way that society would react to the birth of a disabled baby and as such he would *"not find it morally offensive to reflect this difference in an award of compensation."*[19]

- There is a 'significant difference' between disabled parents and disabled children – the disabled parent will eventually benefit from parenthood as their child grows older:

> *"the factors which make it appropriate to award compensation for the birth of a disabled child are present throughout; those which appear to make it appropriate to award damages for the birth of a healthy child to a disabled parent gradually disappear to be overtaken by the advantages."*[20]

18 *Rees v Darlington Memorial Hospital NHS Trust* [2004] 1 A.C. 309 at 346 – 347.

19 *Rees v Darlington Memorial Hospital NHS Trust* [2004] 1 A.C. 309 at 346 and 348.

- The Court of Appeal in *Rees* had not been correct to award the extra maintenance costs associated with the mother's disability, since[21]:

    - It was *"not a legitimate extension of Parkinson, but an illegitimate gloss on McFarlane."*

    - It was *"destructive of the concept of distributive justice."*

    - It was not possible to disentangle the maintenance costs attributable to the parent's disability from those attributable to the birth of the child itself.

    - Waller LJ's concerns in the Court of Appeal were valid and *"principle, common justice and the coherence of the law alike demand that the line be drawn between those costs which are referable to the characteristics of the child and those which are referable to the characteristics of the parent."*

- A conventional award by way of additional general damages was appropriate. He confirmed that this sum would not (and indeed was not intended to) compensate the parents for the costs of raising the child but was awarded to recognise the denial of an *"important aspect of their personal autonomy, viz the right to limit the size of their family"* instead.[22]

<u>Lord Scott of Foscote</u>

Lord Scott of Foscote agreed that the claim for maintenance costs ought to be dismissed, but a conventional sum awarded instead. His decision

---

20 *Ibid.* at 347.

21 *Ibid.* at 348 - 349.

22 *Ibid.* at 349 – 350.

rested on a discussion of the value of human life and the way in which society views a child. His interpretation of *McFarlane* was that it was an exception to normal tortious principles, and he was loath to create an exception to an exception by permitting recovery in *Rees*.

He made the following findings:

- That human life is *"regarded by society generally and by the law as uniquely precious and as incalculable of valuation in money terms."*[23]

- The doctor's negligence was the cause of the maintenance costs being sought: such costs were a reasonably foreseeable consequence of the pregnancy and the pregnancy was what the doctor's services had been engaged to avoid.[24]

- It was reasonable for parents to say that they had no choice but to keep the child and to refuse termination or adoption services.[25]

- *McFarlane* was correctly decided and the departure from normal tortious principles was justified because[26]:

    - The expenses sought as damages were accepted by the parents as *"the price to be paid for having the child as a member of their family."*

    - The value of the child was incapable of proper valuation.

---

23 *Ibid.* at 353.

24 *Ibid.*

25 *Ibid.*

26 *Ibid.* at 354.

- In any event placing a monetary value on the detriment a child brought would be inconsistent with the status of the child as a loved and valued family member.

- The disability of the mother in *Rees* was not sufficient to take the case outside of the exception to normal tortious principles created by *McFarlane* since her baby was also healthy and much loved and *"an exception to an exception is apt to produce messy jurisprudence and ... the creation of an exception in the present case would lead to further exceptions."*[27]

- The decision in *Parkinson* was not consistent with *McFarlane* because:

  - Where the operation was not undertaken with the purpose of avoiding disability, as in *Parkinson*, then there was no justification for treating those cases differently to *McFarlane*. Cases where the purpose of the operation was to avoid disability may need to be treated differently.

  - The difficulties in assessing the balance between the benefits and burdens of a disabled child would be as difficult as in cases concerning healthy children.

  - The birth of a disabled baby was not reasonably foreseeable enough to justify the imposition of damages referable to that disability.

- A conventional award should be awarded to reflect the loss of the expected benefit of a successful operation.[28]

---

27 *Ibid.* at 354 – 355.

28 *Ibid.*

Lord Steyn and Lord Hope of Craighead

Lord Steyn's and Lord Hope of Craighead's judgments are interesting as they also both decided *McFarlane* when it came before the House of Lords. In *Rees* they both provided dissents from the majority and would have awarded the claimant the extra maintenance costs associated with her own disability. They also both endorsed *Parkinson* and did not support the creation of a conventional award.

Lord Steyn

Lord Steyn couched his judgement in corrective justice, and emphasised that one of the key factors in the decision in *McFarlane* had been that the baby was normal and healthy, and that there had been no consideration of the facts which now presented themselves in *Rees* concerning a disabled parent. He considered the most just outcome to be to permit recovery of the extra costs claimed in such cases. He made the following findings:

- That no issues of public policy were considered in *McFarlane* but rather issues of legal policy were determined by examining principles of distributive justice and what was fair, just and reasonable. There were two clear features in the reasoning of *McFarlane*[29]:

    - First, that it was not possible in monetary terms to calculate the benefits of having a child. Hale LJ's analysis of 'deemed equilibrium' in *Parkinson* was not a correct analysis of the way their Lordships had approached this difficulty.

    - That the birth of a normal healthy baby is a blessing and not a detriment.

- That it would not be appropriate for a supreme court of final decision making to depart from *McFarlane* merely because a dif-

29 *Ibid.* at 322.

ferently constituted House of Lords would decide the issue differently.[30]

- *McFarlane* had been decided correctly, despite academic criticism and the subsequent differing decision in the Australian case of *Cattanach v Melchior*.[31] He held that *"the subject is a highly controversial one, the decision of the House, rooted as it was in morality, justice and legal policy, represented the least bad choice"* but was still a sound choice.[32]

- Endorsing *Parkinson* since the *"legal policy on which McFarlane was based is critically dependent on the birth of a healthy and normal child."*[33]

- The extra costs caused by the mother's disability ought to be awarded because[34]:

    - He acknowledged that, to the best of his recollection, their Lordships in *McFarlane* had not considered the case of a disabled parent at all.

    - He agreed with Waller LJ in the Court of Appeal in *Rees* that it was arbitrary to hold that only a parent with disabilities could successfully bring a claim, and it was important for the law to avoid arbitrariness.

    - However, he also found *"great force"* in the judgment of Robert Walker LJ in the Court of Appeal in *Rees*, that disabled people were a category of people whom the law recognised required special considerations.

---

30 *Ibid.* at 324.

31 [2003] HCA 38 (16 July 2003); discussed in further detail in Chapter Twelve.

32 *Rees v Darlington Memorial Hospital NHS Trust* [2004] 1 A.C. 309 at 324.

33 *Ibid.* at 325.

34 *Ibid.* at 326 and 327.

    - Ultimately, he considered that the injustice of denying recovery outweighed the considerations outlined by Waller LJ in his Court of Appeal judgment.

- That the creation of a 'conventional award' ran contrary to principle and amounted to a back-door evasion of the legal policy enunciated in *McFarlane*.[35]

Lord Hope of Craighead

Lord Hope of Craighead's decision rested again on legal policy. He emphasised that the extra maintenance costs associated with disability (whether of a child or of a parent) were possible to calculate and should therefore be awarded directly rather than a conventional sum being awarded in their place. He made the following findings:

- In discussing *McFarlane*[36]:

    - That the critical factor in his decision in *McFarlane* had been the difficulty in calculating damages: if calculation was impossible then it must be held to fall outside of the duty of care.

    - That he did not base his decision on the belief that it was morally repugnant to award damages for a healthy child as *"the fundamental value which is attached to human life is an ethical, not an economic, concept and the problem which had to be addressed was legal, not theological."*

    - That Hale LJ's 'deemed equilibrium' analysis was not correct and that instead it had been decided that any attempt at such a calculation was impossible.

---

35 *Ibid.* at 327 – 328.

36 *Ibid.* at 328 and 330.

- That the issues which arose in *Parkinson* presented a separate question to those determined by *McFarlane* and that as a matter of legal policy the Court of Appeal in *Parkinson* was correct to award damages for the additional maintenance costs associated with the child's disability.[37]

- That although some may criticise the decision to award a disabled parent extra maintenance costs associated with that disability and although there may be difficulties in calculating those extra costs, such costs should still be awarded due to *"the inescapable fact that the seriously disabled parent cannot, however hard she tries, do all the things that a normal, healthy parent can do when carrying out the ordinary tasks involved in a child's upbringing."*[38]

- There was no risk of disability discrimination being a consequence of the decision to award damages to disabled parents since[39]:

    - Legislation already recognised the fact of disability and the risk of discrimination and disadvantage that it gave rise to, and that *"the respect and value which the law places on every life extends to everybody irrespective of whether they are born with or without disabilities."*

    - In permitting recovery for the extra maintenance costs associated with disability the law will be *"doing its best"* to enable the disabled parent to perform their tasks as parent *"on equal terms"* with those who are not disabled.

- That a conventional award was not appropriate as[40]:

---

37 *Ibid.* at 329 and 330.

38 *Ibid.* at 331 and 332.

39 *Ibid.* at 332.

40 *Ibid.* at 333 – 335.

- A conventional sum of money was normally awarded where there was *"no pecuniary guideline which can point the way to a correct assessment."*

- A conventional sum should not be awarded where, as here, the financial loss was capable of assessment in money terms and fell within a head of special damages.

- The creation of a conventional award was contrary to normal tortious principles.

- There was no consistent or coherent ratio to support the award within the speeches of the majority.

- To apply the conventional award equally across all cases regardless of the disability of the parent or child was not appropriate where calculation of the extra costs in these cases was possible: it was an "*over-statement*" to describe quantification of these losses as acutely difficult.

Lord Hutton

Lord Hutton provided the final dissent to the decision of the majority. He relied on the *Caparo* test like many of their Lordships before him and was of the view that the House of Lords in *McFarlane* had created an exception to the normal principles of tortious recovery and that that exception should not apply where the child or mother was disabled. [41]

He made the following findings:

- That the decision in *McFarlane* was decided correctly, but that even if it was not then he would still not depart from it. [42]

41 See more discussion of the way their Lordships in *McFarlane* approached the *Caparo* test in Chapter Five.

42 *Rees v Darlington Memorial Hospital NHS Trust* [2004] 1 A.C. 309 at 338.

- The House of Lords in *McFarlane* did acknowledge that *"on normal principles of tort law the claim for the cost of bringing up the child would succeed"* but the 'fundamental principle' underlying the decision was that it would not be fair, just and reasonable to award maintenance costs.[43]

- The Court of Appeal in *Parkinson* was correct to award the extra maintenance costs associated with the child's disability and that such extra costs ought to be awarded where the parent themselves is disabled because[44]:

    - It is not unjust, unfair or unreasonable to award damages for the extra costs of bringing up a child where the mother is disabled.

    - There is a clear distinction between healthy and disabled parents which ought to be recognised.

    - *"McFarlane created an exception to the general principles, that that exception does not apply to a disabled child or a disabled mother, and that accordingly the McFarlane decision does not bar the mother from recovering in this case."*

The majority decision of the House of Lords was therefore to deny the claim for maintenance costs in the case of disabled parents, but to also create a new 'conventional award' of £15,000 to be applied to all cases (not just those involving disabled parents) by way of inflated general damages to reflect the legal wrong suffered by claimants in such cases.

---

43 *Ibid.*

44 *Ibid.* at 340 and 342.

Summary

Rees again threw the reasoning of the House of Lords in *McFarlane* under the microscope, this time in a case involving a disabled parent of a healthy child born as a result of a negligent sterilisation. Once again the House of Lords were in a difficult position, having to re-asses an area of law which had only come before the House very recently. Lord Bingham of Cornhill and Lord Millett even suggested that before they had even considered the merits of the decision in *McFarlane* they felt bound to uphold it given the strict tests which apply where the House of Lords is deciding whether to depart from one of its own previous decisions and because insufficient time had lapsed between *McFarlane* and the judgments they were now delivering in *Rees*.

The facts in *Rees* cast under a spotlight many of the concerns which were raised in *McFarlane* and which resulted in the decision to deny recovery. The fact that a claim had been brought by a disabled parent challenged arguments regarding the incalculable benefits of parenthood and fears of over-compensating a claimant, since the benefits of parenthood arguably diminish where a parent is disabled and unable to care for their healthy child without greater personal and financial disadvantage. *Rees* also satisfied arguments regarding foreseeability to a greater extent than *McFarlane* since the parent was disabled at the time of negligence and, particularly where the operation was undertaken specifically to avoid the difficulties and costs associated with raising a child whilst disabled, the defendant was aware at the time of the operation what the consequences would be were that operation performed negligently. Foreseeability in cases like *Rees* is actually less problematic than in cases like *Parkinson*, where there is an award made due to the disability of the child, but that disability was not itself caused by any negligence. Even so the House of Lords did not consider that the facts in *Rees* warranted any change in the law or further development of the principles set down in *McFarlane*, save for the creation of a new head of loss in the form of the conventional award.

The support of the House of Lords for a conventional award, developed from Lord Millett's initial suggestion in *McFarlane* itself, demonstrates the unwillingness of the majority to leave a claimant who has suffered a legal wrong without remedy, particularly since the conventional award appears to be intended regardless of the health of the parents or child. However, even the creation of this conventional award was not uncontroversial. Lord Bingham and Lord Millet both expressly stated that the conventional award was not intended to be compensatory in a special damages sense, but was simply an award of damages akin to general damages. The minority however felt that this conventional award marked a departure from the decision in *McFarlane*, ran contrary to principle and was not appropriate where it related to a head of damages which was properly capable of calculation. Lord Bingham of Cornhill suggests that the conventional award is simply a 'gloss' on the previous *McFarlane* ruling, but if that is the case then it is not clear why Lord Millett's initial suggestion in *McFarlane* did not gain acceptance when it was first suggested nor is it consistent with the fact that Lord Steyn and Lord Hope of Craighead (both also Law Lords who delivered judgments in *McFarlane*) are critical of the creation of a such an award.

The result of both *Parkinson*[45] and *Rees* was that the decision in *McFarlane* was modified to afford claimants limited recovery in wrongful conception claims. Since these cases there has been little, if any, disruption to the status quo. It is clear however that there do remain some unanswered questions as to the scope of recovery in such claims. In particular it is not clear from the judgments in *Rees* to what extent the principles laid down in *McFarlane* would be applicable to wrongful birth claims (as opposed to wrongful conception claims which is the type of claim that *McFarlane*, *Parkinson* and *Rees* addressed), with obiter comment in the key cases regarding wrongful birth actions raising different policy questions. It is also unclear the extent to which *Parkinson* remains good law and whether a different outcome would be reached were a case with similar facts to come before the House of Lords, given the criticism the decision faced from some of their Lordships in *Rees*. There have been recent challenges to the decision of the House of Lords in *Rees*; these are examined further in Chapter Nine.

45 Discussed in detail in Chapter Six.

Although many of their Lordships in *Rees* expressed the view that *McFarlane* had been decided correctly, there also appeared to be a general reluctance to re-visit the decision at all given how recently *McFarlane* had been heard by the House of Lords. Certainly, it seemed that the Court of Appeal in *Parkinson* might have reached a different decision than in *McFarlane* had they not been bound by *McFarlane* as superior authority. Enough time has perhaps now passed for wrongful conception and wrongful birth cases to be re-considered by the Supreme Court and a different decision reached without this being perceived as see-saw law making. Of course, any re-examination of the issues by the Supreme Court would be subject to the usual strict tests which are applied in cases where the Supreme Court is being asked to re-visit one of its own decisions.[46] Were the matter to come back before the Supreme Court then lessons could be learned from the resolution of these very same issues in legal systems abroad, which are examined further in Chapter Twelve.

46 See Lord Steyn's and Lord Hutton's judgments in *Rees v Darlington Memorial Hospital NHS Trust* [2004] 1 A.C. 309 at 323 and 338. A fuller discussion of the relevant authorities is outside the scope of this book.

CHAPTER EIGHT
RECENT DEVELOPMENTS: WRONGFUL LIFE

<u>Introduction</u>

There have been no substantive challenges to *McKay v Essex Area Health Authority and Another*[1] since the House of Lords delivered judgment over 35 years ago, although there have been some recent cases in lower courts which refer to, and appear to affirm, the House of Lords decision in *McKay*.[2]

<u>Criminal Injuries Compensation Authority v First Tier Tribunal (Social Entitlement Chamber)</u>

The Facts and Earlier Decisions

There was recent judicial discussion of *McKay* in *Criminal Injuries Compensation Authority v First Tier Tribunal (Social Entitlement Chamber)*.[3] Here a claim was made for criminal injuries compensation by a child born with a genetic disorder, who was conceived following the incestuous rape of his mother. The child's mother had herself received compensation under the *Criminal Injuries Compensation Scheme 2008*, following a protracted period of rape by her father (who had pleaded guilty to incest) and the subsequent birth of two children, one of whom was the child in this action who had been born with a genetic disorder.[4]

---

1 [1982] 2 Q.B. 1166; discussed in full in Chapter Three.

2 As well as the two cases discussed here see also *Whitehead v Searle* [2008] EWCA Civ 285, [2009] 1 W.L.R. 549, discussed in detail in Chapter Nine.

3 [2017] EWCA Civ 139; [2017] 4 WLR 60.

4 [2017] 4 WLR 60 at p1.

The claim came before the Court of Appeal following a number of earlier decisions as follows:

- The Criminal Injuries Compensation Authority (CICA) refused the child's claim on the basis that he was not a victim of a crime of violence; this decision was maintained even after review.[5]

- On appeal, the First Tier Tribunal (FTT) held that the child had not suffered injury within the terms of the scheme[6]:

    - To treat the child's conception and birth as injury for the purposes of the scheme was to treat the claim as one for wrongful life since his actionable injury was his having been born at all.

    - The common law does not recognise a claim for wrongful life, per *McKay* which was *"unchallenged authority."*

    - The scheme was free-standing, but regard could still be had to the relevant common law if appropriate to do so, and at common law the child would have no claim (although his mother *"would have a claim for certain additional costs of bringing up a disabled child"*).

    - It would be impossible to quantify the child's claim: there were difficulties with defining the injury, placing his condition on the tariff of awards and finding a benchmark against which to assess loss of earnings.

    - It was implausible that the scheme would provide far greater recovery from public funds than would be available under the common law.

---

5 *Ibid.* at p2.

6 *Ibid.* at p2 – p4.

- The Upper Tribunal heard a judicial review application of the FTT's decision. Judge Levenson reversed the earlier decisions and awarded the child compensation. He held that the development of the law in relation to wrongful life claims was of limited assistance, holding that the scheme was intended to be a self-contained scheme which was not to be influenced by common law developments. He held that there was no provision in the scheme that at the time that the crime of violence was committed the applicant must have been 'a person' and that *"in common parlance"* the child had suffered injuries which were attributable to a crime of violence.[7]

CICA then appealed the Upper Tribunal's decision, which was heard by the Court of Appeal.

The Court of Appeal Decision

The Court of Appeal upheld the appeal and rejected the child's claim for compensation. The lead judgment was delivered by Sir Brian Leveson P, with which McFarlane LJ and Henderson LJJ agreed.[8] The claim was rejected for the following reasons:

- The scheme was now governed by Section 1 of the *Criminal Injuries Act 1995* and was governed by the rules of statutory construction.
- The scheme no longer assessed damages by reference to common law principles but on a prescribed tariff instead.
- The only victim of the crime, under the terms of the scheme, was the mother:
    - The child could not be the victim of a crime committed before he was conceived.

---

7 *Ibid.* at p4 – p5.

8 *Ibid.* at p6 – p7.

    - Paragraph 9(c) of the scheme provides that compensation will not be payable in respect of a sexual offence unless the applicant was the non-consenting victim of that offence.

- It was not possible to calculate compensation in any event, and to calculate damages on the basis that the child would otherwise have been born without a disability went beyond what the scheme sought to cover.

- It was *"difficult to see why, as a matter of fairness, the common law approach"* to the mother's right to claim damages for the costs of caring for a disabled child, illustrated in *Parkinson v St James and Seacroft University Hospital NHS Trust,*[9] should not be incorporated in to the scheme.

Henderson LJ also emphasised that a claim for wrongful life could not be successful in English law, holding that:

> *"... his real complaint would have to be that he should never have been conceived at all. A complaint of that nature, however is not a claim for personal injury, but a claim for wrongful existence, which as this court explained in McKay v Essex Area Health Authority [1982] Q.B. 1166 is not one which the law can recognise, or for which compensation could be assessed."*

Commentary

The re-iteration by the Court of Appeal of the principles set out in *McKay* is perhaps unsurprising given that *Mckay* is a House of Lords decision and so the Court of Appeal was bound by it. Nonetheless the court still expressly referenced *McKay* and appear to be cognisant to reach a decision consistent with it. Additionally, the same difficulties expressed in *McKay* in respect of calculating damages were set out in this recent case and were relied on to deny the child's claim. This sug-

9 [2001] EWCA Civ 530; discussed in full in Chapter Six.

gests that the mood of the court when presented with a wrongful life claim remains the same as 35 years ago when *McKay* was heard.

The discussion of *Parkinson* in this case is also interesting. As is discussed in previous chapters, following *Rees* there was some question as to the extent to which *Parkinson* remained good law.[10] Although the court was bound by *Parkinson* in any event, the instant case does still appear to affirm as good law the outcome of *Parkinson,* by expressly suggesting that the principles set out in *Parkinson* should be mirrored by the compensation the scheme itself provides.

TBS v Commissioner of Police of the Metropolis

The Facts and the Decision

McKay has also been recently discussed in a strike out application heard in the High Court, in the case of *TBS v Commissioner of Police of the Metropolis.*[11] A claimant, who had been conceived as a result of a fraudulent sexual relationship between his mother and an undercover police officer, brought a personal injury claim for damages, alleging that he had suffered from psychiatric injury as a result of learning that he had been conceived in such a relationship.[12]

The claimant's mother was a political activist, who a police officer had engaged in a relationship with as part of an undercover operation. As a result, the claimant was conceived and born, and the police officer was present in a paternal role for the first three years of his life before abandoning him with no explanation. The police officer's true identity and role was later discovered by the claimant and his mother. The claimant alleged that because of the deceptive conduct of the police officer, which resulted in his conception, birth and subsequent aban-

---

10 See Chapter Seven.

11 [2017] EWHC 3094 (Q.B.).

12 *Ibid.* at [1] – [6].

donment, he had suffered from psychiatric injury in the form of an adjustment disorder.[13]

The claimant brought a claim for damages against the police commissioner, both on the basis of misfeasance in public office and, of more interest here, negligence. The claimant argued that he was owed a duty of care because the defendant and his officers ought to have known that there were obvious risks that a child would be conceived during the undercover operation and that harm would be caused to any child so conceived. The defendant applied to strike out the claim: with respect to the claim in negligence the defendant argued that the claimant's claim was one for wrongful life, which was contrary to public policy as it offended the sanctity of life.[14]

Nicol J dismissed the strike out application in respect of the claim in negligence. He held that this was not a wrongful life case and *McKay* could be distinguished. He did not consider that the claimant was seeking compensation for having been born at all, but rather that he was seeking compensation for the psychiatric damage he alleged he had suffered as a result of the conduct of the police officer towards him and his mother: his claim was not that he should never have been born, but that he had suffered psychiatric injury due to the circumstances of his father. Nicol J did not consider the claimant's claim, framed in this way, offended the sanctity of life and further held that it was also far from certain that the claimant would fail to establish that he was owed a duty of care and so was entitled to compensation for the harm which had foreseeably flowed from the breach of that duty. He was therefore not content to strike out the claim.[15]

Commentary

The way *McKay* was distinguished from these facts provides insight in to the way in which some wrongful life style actions may be capable of

13 *Ibid.*

14 *Ibid.* at [1] – [6] and [36] – [37].

15 *Ibid.* at [37] – [40].

succeeding, though it is difficult to imagine a set of facts in a clinical negligence setting which would be distinguishable from *McKay* in the same way as here.

The reasoning in this case is also open to argument. The Judge here stated that one of the differences between this case and *McKay* was that in *McKay* but for the negligence the claimant child would never have been born, but that that was not so in this case. However, part of the claim in negligence related to permitting the undercover police officer to engage in sexual relations with the claimant's mother and so arguably, but for the negligence in this case the claimant would never have existed either (as if the police officer had not been permitted to engage in sexual relations with the mother the claimant would never have been conceived). This was of course only one part of the alleged negligence and the whole course of conduct of the police officer formed part of the claim, including actions following the claimant's birth, which may be what stands this case apart from *McKay*.

As this was a strike out application heard in December 2017 it will be interesting to see how this case is eventually argued at trial and what the outcome is, if it progresses that far.

Summary

There has been no substantive wrongful life case heard by a senior court since the decision handed down by the House of Lords in *McKay* in 1982. Very recently, and after a long period of no judicial activity at all, there have been two cases which have discussed *McKay*, though neither were final trial judgments. The Court of Appeal, hearing a CICA appeal, appeared to affirm *McKay* and delivered a judgment on recovery of compensation under the scheme which was consistent with the principles set out in *McKay*.

A strike out application in respect of a claim which was framed in very similar terms to a wrongful life action was dismissed and *McKay* was distinguished. Although that case raises interesting questions about the ways in which the bar to recover in *McKay* may be avoided, it is unlikely to have any real practical application in a clinical negligence setting and was not a final judgment on the matter.

The case of *Whitehead*, which is discussed in full in Chapter Nine, also appeared to affirm the decision in *McKay*, holding that the child left without the benefit of his mother's or father's claim was still not permitted to bring a claim in his own right.

There has undoubtedly been a shift in the way that society and the courts address issues relating to the sanctity of life, with a greater acceptance that in some circumstances it is in the best interests of an individual to die.[16] Although these recent cases appear to affirm *McKay* they do at least involve discussion of the issues explored in *McKay* for the first time in quite a while. It remains to be seen whether the door has opened to a re-assessment of wrongful life claims by the Supreme Court.

---

16 Discussed in more detail in Chapter Thirteen.

CHAPTER NINE
RECENT DEVELOPMENTS: WRONGFUL CONCEPTION AND WRONGFUL BIRTH

Introduction

There have been very few reported wrongful conception and wrongful birth cases since the decision in *Rees v Darlington Memorial Hospital NHS Trust.*[1] The law has been treated as settled for some time, with no change to the status quo which *Rees* established. However as can be seen from previous chapters the progression of wrongful conception and wrongful birth actions through the courts have left open some issues as to the scope and extent of recovery.

Recent cases have presented challenges to the established legal position. These cases have explored important issues on which a determination from the Supreme Court is still required, including the rights of a father, the recoverability of damages where an action is brought in contract rather than tort and the extent of the recoverability of damages where a child is born disabled.

Wrongful Conception

A recent wrongful conception case attracted media interest due to its controversial facts. This case explored, amongst other interesting aspects, the extent to which the principles in relation to the recoverability of damages in wrongful conception claims brought in tort applied to claims brought under contract.

ARB v IVF Hammersmith and R[2] involved a claim was brought against an IVF clinic by a father following an alleged forgery of a consent form

1 [2004] 1 A.C. 309; discussed in full in Chapter Seven.

2 [2017] EWHC 2438 (Q.B.).

which led to the implantation of an embryo without the claimant's consent, and subsequent birth of an 'unwanted child'. The cause of action was in contract and, although successful on liability, the claimant was refused damages on the grounds that policy considerations precluded an award of damages for the maintenance costs of the child.

ARB v IVF Hammersmith and R

The Facts

The claimant was in a relationship with the third party to the action, R. They had previously undergone one cycle of IVF with the defendant clinic in 2008, following which a son had been born. At that time the claimant had signed documents which first, acknowledged that he had been provided with sufficient information about the options for treatment and that he understood he could change or withdraw his consent at any time, and second, that provided for the storage of the embryos for up to 10 years. Both the claimant and R signed documents which stated that they understood they both needed to give consent for the thawing and replacement of embryos and that they had an obligation to inform the clinic of any material change in their circumstances.[3]

In March 2010 the couple returned to the IVF clinic for advice. At some point the claimant and R were provided with a Consent to the Thawing of Embryos Form ('the Consent Form'). Unfortunately, shortly after the visit to the IVF clinic the relationship between the claimant and R broke down and R moved out. R continued to undergo treatment at the clinic however with a view to the implantation of a further embryo. The claimant's case was that he had no knowledge of and did not consent to this. The claimant alleged that he had never signed this form and that R must have forged his signature.[4] An embryo was thawed and successfully implanted in November 2010; R only

3 *Ibid.* at [2] and [8] – [16].

4 *Ibid.* at [2] – [3] and [17] – [19].

informed the claimant that she was pregnant in February 2011 and she gave birth to a healthy baby girl in the summer of that same year.[5]

Following a number of complaints both to the clinic and to the Human Fertilisation and Embryology Authority ('HFEA') the claimant instituted legal proceedings. He claimed that in going ahead with the implantation of an embryo without his consent the defendant was in breach of contract, whether by way of an express or implied term in the contract. He claimed damages which included a substantial claim for the maintenance costs of his daughter.[6]

The defendant argued that the extent of the clinic's obligation was an implied term to exercise reasonable care in obtaining the claimant's consent and complying with the terms of its license and the *Human Fertilisation and Embryology Act 1990* (the '1990 Act'). The defendant denied that there had been a breach of contract and in the alternative alleged that there could be no liability in any event (or at least must be a reduction for contributory negligence) due to the claimant's own breach in failing to inform the clinic that his relationship had broken down. Further the defendant argued that no award of damages could be made pursuant to legal policy and / or that such damages were too remote.[7]

The defendant also brought Part 20 proceedings against R for an indemnity, relying on the tort of deceit.[8]

The Decision: Liability

The claim was heard by Jay J He preferred the evidence of the claimant as to the history of the matter and that he had no intention of having another child with R, and he was persuaded by the evidence of a handwriting expert that the signature on the Consent Form was not a genuine signature of the claimant. He therefore found that R had

---

5 *Ibid.* at [20] – [27] and [47].

6 *Ibid.* at [155].

7 *Ibid.* at [156].

8 *Ibid.* at [4] and [157].

forged the claimant's signature as alleged. As the claimant had not therefore provided his signature he could not be said to have provided valid informed consent to the implantation of an embryo. He also held that the claimant had not been provided with sufficient information to enable him to provide consent in any event.[9]

It then fell for Jay J to determine, in those circumstances, what the extent of the duty owed to the claimant under the contract was and whether such duty had been breached. He made the following findings:

- There was an implied term in the contract that the defendant would comply with its obligations under the 1990 Act, HFEA Guidance and the clinic's license conditions, at the time consent was being sought for the thawing and replacement of an embryo[10]:
    - This implied term was not however a strict duty but rather amounted to a duty to exercise reasonable care.
    - On the evidence he did not consider that this term had been breached, applying the usual *Bolam / Bolitho* tests.[11]
    - This conclusion was based on the following:
        i. Evidence that the defendant's practices and procedures were considered common place at the time the negligence occurred.
        ii. HFEA's Code of Practice contemplated treatment where partners did not attend the clinic.

---

9 *Ibid.* at [167] – [210].

10 *Ibid.* at [215] – [246], [262] and [273] – [283].

11 See Chapter Two for more discussion on the standard of care in clinical negligence cases.

iii. R had continued to behave as though the claimant was involved in and informed about the treatment.

iv. The clinic was entitled to believe that the claimant had signed a patient questionnaire on the date that document bore (this was a separate document to the Consent Form and was dated much later than the March consultation and closer to the date the embryo was implanted).

- There was an express term in the contract, that the defendant clinic would not thaw and implant an embryo without the claimant's prior written consent. This imposed a strict duty on the defendant and this duty had been breached. On this basis he found in the claimant's favour on liability.[12]

- Although the claimant had also breached the contract by failing to inform the defendant of the breakdown of his relationship he was not persuaded that factual causation in respect of this breach had been properly pleaded or established on the evidence.[13]

The Decision: Public Policy and the Recoverability of Damages

The fact that there had been a breach of duty under the contract did not automatically entitle the claimant to an award of damages and Jay J was then required to address the recoverability of the damages claimed. He found that there could be no difference between tortious and contractual claims founded on identical substantive duties and the damages claimed were not recoverable.[14]

---

12 *ARB v IVF Hammersmith and R* [2017] EWHC 2438 (Q.B.).

13 *Ibid.* at [273] – [287].

14 *Ibid.* at [288] – [323].

He considered the previous cases of *McFarlane v Tayside Health Board*[15] and *Rees v Darlington Memorial Hospital NHS Trust*[16] but found that, although three of their Lordships in *McFarlane* had touched on claims which were brought in contract, none determined the issue and their judgments were specifically tied to the tort of negligence, and that the ratio in *Rees* was also limited to tortious claims.[17]

Jay J felt that the issue of recoverability of damages required further consideration and held that *"the public policy bar would apply to the contractual claim if there were relevant equivalence or congruence with a hypothetical claim in tort brought on the same facts."*[18] He held that there was sufficient congruence to treat a contractual claim based on breach of a duty to act with reasonable care and a contractual claim based on breach of a strict duty (as here) in the same way since[19]:

- The measure of damages is the same, whichever way the claim is brought.
- The test for remoteness does not turn on any distinction which relates to the underlying obligation.
- There is no material difference for the purposes of legal policy between contractual duties of those two types.

He held that there were clear legal policy objections to permitting an award of damages for the maintenance costs of a healthy child, which included:

- The inherent difficulty, if not impossibility, of measuring the loss.

15 [2000] 2 A.C. 59; discussed in full in Chapter Five.

16 [2004] 1 A.C. 309; discussed in full in Chapter Seven.

17 [2017] EWHC 2338 (Q.B.) at [290] – [304].

18 *Ibid.* at [305].

19 *Ibid.* at [305] – [318].

- An unwillingness to regard a healthy child as solely a financial liability.

- The refusal to offset the benefits which accrue from parenthood from any financial liabilities.

- A feeling that a claim for such damages was morally unacceptable.

- That it was not fair, just or reasonable, to allow this sort of claim.

He considered that most of the policy considerations applied even where the contractual duty was strict and that he had *"difficulty with the notion that a private patient could succeed where an NHS patient could not."*[20] He was not persuaded that *Rees* could be distinguished on the present facts and left open the question as to whether the claimant would be successful in a claim for a conventional award, as was established by *Rees*.[21]

Finally, he held that the law on remoteness of damage did not, in principle, bar the claimant's claim but the individual elements of his claim would require further examination in future were that found to be necessary.[22] He relied on *H. Parsons (Livestock) Ltd v Uttley Ingham & Co Ltd*[23] as authority for treating the question of remoteness of damage in the same way, regardless of whether the claim is brought in contract or tort, where the duties relied on are identical (and he held that it was immaterial whether the contractual duty relied on was strict or to take reasonable care).[24]

---

20 *Ibid.* [319].

21 *Ibid.* at [320] – [322].

22 *Ibid.* at [324] – [340].

23 [1978] 1 Q.B. 791, cited by *ARB v IVF Hammersmith and R* [2017] EWHC 2438 (Q.B.) at [309] onwards.

24 [2017] EWHC 2338 at [309] – [317].

Commentary

An appeal is outstanding on the decision in this interesting case. It means that the Court of Appeal will be re-visiting the question of the recoverability of damages in wrongful conception and wrongful birth cases, something which has not been done for over 15 years. Practitioners should watch this case with keen interest as the way in which the Court of Appeal approaches the issue will likely have an impact on whether further cases are advanced in these areas or whether it is an area of law which will fall quiet once again.

If *IVF Hammersmith* ends up in the Supreme Court, then it will be the first time since *Rees* that the Supreme Court has been asked to re-visit the law in relation to wrongful conception and wrongful birth claims. Although it would be an uphill battle to do so, the Supreme Court may even be asked to amend the law in relation to the recoverability of damages; at the very least there would be an opportunity for the Supreme Court to clarify some of the outstanding questions regarding the scope and extent of recoverability in these cases. *IVF Hammersmith* is therefore a case which presents a potential disruption to an area of law which has remained settled for a long time.[25]

Wrongful Birth

Those cases which have been determined by the senior courts these have primarily been in relation to wrongful conception, as opposed to wrongful birth, claims.[26] However, there have been two notable claims regarding wrongful birth, one heard less recently but coming before the Court of Appeal, and one having been heard very recently in the High Court. These claims have explored important issues which the key cases left open, namely the extent to which a claim may survive following a

25 See Chapter Thirteen for a discussion on the likelihood of a change in the law.

26 With the exception of *Groom v Selby* [2001] EWCA Civ 1522, a wrongful birth claim heard by the Court of Appeal following *Parkinson v St James and Seacroft University Hospital NHS Trust* [2001] EWCA Civ 530; both discussed in Chapter Six.

mother's death and the rights of a father to bring a stand-alone claim, as well as the reach of the decision in *Parkinson v St James and Seacroft University Hospital NHS Trust*[27] and the types of claim in which the extra maintenance costs associated with disability will be found to be recoverable.

Whitehead v Searle

The Facts and First Instance Decision

Whitehead[28] involved a professional negligence action, brought by the ex-partner of a deceased mother (primarily on behalf of her estate but also in his personal capacity) who had been bringing a wrongful birth claim for maintenance costs, against the deceased's solicitors. The ex-partner was also the father of the child who was the subject of the wrongful birth claim. In the mother's original action she was likely to have been successful in her claim for some maintenance costs since her child had been born with a disability and so the case was subject to the exception established in *Parkinson*; the allegation was that clinicians had failed to diagnose spina bifida in the foetus during the mother's pregnancy and so had frustrated the mother's ability to elect to undergo a termination.[29]

The solicitors who had been acting on behalf of the mother had not concluded the matter before she died, and consequently the right to recover the additional maintenance costs had died with her (since it was accepted that the measure of her claim for damages could not extend to any loss or expense incurred after death); had the matter been concluded before she had died then the losses would have extended to cover the additional maintenance costs into the future. The action against the mother's solicitors was for those lost recoverable costs.[30]

---

27 [2001] EWCA Civ 530; Discussed in full in Chapter Six.

28 [2008] EWCA Civ 285, [2009] 1 W.L.R. 549; Also known as *McLeish (Deceased), Re Hibbert Pownall & Newton (A Firm) v Whitehead*.

29 [2009] 1 W.L.R. 549 at 549.

30 *Ibid.* at 555 – 556.

The decision at first instance was that the defendant firm was liable for the maintenance costs for the benefit of the mother's estate. The father's claim in his personal capacity was dismissed on the basis that the legal representatives of the mother did not owe the father a duty of care.[31] The basis of that decision was that the father himself had no claim against the health authority. The Judge was prepared to accept that a *"husband or co-habitee father may have a claim for damages … any such claim would have to be subject to the proviso that it is linked to that of the mother of the child."*[32] He then clarified that to be linked to a mother's claim it must have been reasonably foreseeable that a breach of duty to the mother would result in losses to the father as well; as the father in *Whitehead* had been somewhat absent (not living with the mother and making only occasional contributions to the upbringing of the child) the Judge was not satisfied that the father met that hurdle.[33]

The Court of Appeal Decision

On appeal the first instance decision was overturned.

In respect of the claim on behalf of the estate (brought by the father in his representative capacity) the Court of Appeal found that to award damages to the estate would present an uncovenanted windfall and would therefore go further than what the law would normally allow the father to recover in his representative capacity. This was because the mother's claim for the future maintenance costs of the child died with her: the law entitled the mother, and now her estate, to claim for losses incurred during her lifetime and these maintenance costs could not be recovered by the estate as they would now not be incurred by the mother.[34]

In respect of the father's claim in his personal capacity, counsel for the defendant solicitors firm argued that there was no established cause of

---

31 *Ibid.* at 555.

32 *Ibid.* at 568; [2007] EWHC 1060 (Q.B.) at [94].

33 *Ibid.* at 568; [2007] EWHC 1060 (Q.B.) at [94] – [106].

34 *Ibid.* at 557 – 562 and 574 – 578.

action for a father in a wrongful birth or wrongful conception claim. The Court of Appeal, like the Judge at first instance, addressed the extent to which the father had a claim in his own right against the health authority[35]:

- Laws LJ was of the view that such a claim would be *"viable, if at all, only as a secondary claim"* and that it would face important difficulties (including policy considerations).

- Rix LJ was more optimistic about the right of a father to bring such a claim, he stated that:

    - Such a claim was a *"potentially difficult but realistically arguable claim."*

    - He did not think it could be said that there was *"no real chance of a father showing that a duty of care was owed to him as well as to the mother at the time when the negligence resulting in a wrongful birth occurred."* He gave an example of a mother dying in childbirth and the father then solely bearing the maintenance costs of the child as the type of case where such a duty might be found to exist.

    - Although accepting that the law did not allow the child himself to bring a claim he did not consider that this led to the conclusion that it was not fair, just and reasonable to *"give proper consideration to whether a father's undertaking of the care of the child, in the absence of a deceased mother, should not, in part out of concern for the child himself, be made the occasion for a claim."*

These views did not however take him as far as a dissent. Ultimately, he held that the potential existence of such a claim was insufficient to establish a duty of care owed directly to the father

35 *Ibid.*: Laws LJ at 562 – 569, Rix LJ at 569 – 574, Rimer LJ at 574 - 578.

by the defendant solicitors firm, and so the professional negligence claim by the father in his personal capacity failed.

- Both the judgments of Laws LJ and Rix LJ suggested that although fathers might have a cause of action this was by no means an established right and the extent of such a right was uncertain in any event (such that even if a cause of action did exist it may still be parasitic on the mother's own claim).

- Rimer LJ agreed with Laws LJ's reasoning in dismissing the father's claim in his personal capacity. He did not add anything further with respect to that aspect of the appeal or to the discussion surrounding the potential for a father to bring a wrongful birth or wrongful conception claim in his own right.

Accordingly, the Court of Appeal also dismissed the father's claim in his own personal capacity.

Laws LJ was also clear that the child himself had no cause of action, per *McKay*, holding that the gap in the law which exists because of the absence of a cause of action for the child is *"left advisedly"* and that it was the court's duty to leave that gap unfilled.[36]

This meant that there was no successful claim for maintenance costs at all and, although the child would have benefitted from the award of damages for maintenance costs which would have been awarded to the mother had her claim been settled during her lifetime, that same child was now left with no damages at all.

Commentary

The maintenance costs in *Whitehead* did not simply disappear on the death of the mother, they remain and must be met by someone. The only way the losses can be recovered, in the absence of a mother to bring the claim, is either under an action for wrongful life made by the

---

36 Ibid. at 567.

child itself or a claim brought by the person left with the burden of caring for the child (and thereby incurring those costs) in place of the mother. However, it has long been established that an action for wrongful life will not succeed[37] and the decision in *Whitehead* shows that it is far from settled law that an action brought by anyone other than the mother for maintenance costs would be successful, notwithstanding the fact that those losses have only been incurred as a result of negligence.

The Court in *Whitehead* appeared reticent to accept that fathers may well have the right to bring a claim for maintenance costs. That the Court was not willing to readily accept this concept sits slightly at odds with previous wrongful birth / conception claims where losses have been sought by both parents. The leading cases appear to accept fathers as having a right of action. *McFarlane v Tayside Health Board* involved a claim made by both parents in respect of maintenance costs; although that claim was of course denied the focus was certainly not on refusing to allow the father to claim, but rather on the recoverability of such costs generally. [38] In *Parkinson v St James and Seacroft University Hospital NHS Trust* Hale LJ made obiter remarks as to the rights of a father in such claims; she was of the *"tentative view ... that if there is a sufficient relationship of proximity between the tortfeasor and the father who not only has but meets his parental responsibility to care for the child"* then the father would be able to bring a claim in his own right. [39]

In *McLelland v Greater Glasgow Health Board,*[40] a case which very closely followed *McFarlane*, the defendant accepted that a duty of care was owed to the father as well as the mother and it was admitted that, as the child had been born with Down's syndrome, the maintenance costs associated with the disability were recoverable by both. The same was

37 *McKay v Essex Area Health Authority and Another* [1982] 2 Q.B. 1166; discussed in full in Chapter Three.

38 [2000] 2 A.C. 59; discussed in full in Chapter Five.

39 [2001] EWCA Civ 530; discussed in full in Chapter Six.

40 [2001] S.L.T 446.

evident in the cases of *Salih v Enfield*[41] and *Rand v East Dorset Health Authority*[42] where both parents made claims which succeeded. In *Anderson v Forth Valley Health Board*[43] the court went further, making an express statement that a duty of care was owed to the father as much to the mother since it was clear that both he and his wife would be affected by the pregnancy and its consequences. The court in *Anderson* was however keen to show that such a principle had limits, stating that the duty would only arise where it could be reasonably expected that the father would be involved in the upbringing of the child to a significant degree.

What is clear from *Whitehead* is that there is still judicial debate to be had regarding the rights of a father to claim for maintenance costs in wrongful conception and wrongful birth actions. Laws LJ was certainly of the view that the law in this respect was still developing and that the matter ought to be authoritatively concluded in a case calling for its decision; he did not consider *Whitehead* to be such a case. *Whitehead* was of course a professional negligence case as opposed to a stand-alone claim by the father in a wrongful birth / conception action, and so different considerations applied to the determination of liability. Nevertheless, the judgments of Laws LJ and Rix LJ make express comment on the rights of a father in wrongful conception and wrongful birth claims, and the matter is very much left open.

Whitehead is also another recent case to comment on *McKay* and affirm it, in this case even refusing to permit the child to bring a claim for maintenance costs where, but for the death of his mother he would otherwise have had the benefit of those very same damages.[44]

---

41 [1991] 3 All ER 400.

42 [2000] Lloyd's Rep. Med. 181.

43 [1998] S.L.T. 588.

44 [2009] 1 W.L.R. 549, see Laws LJ's judgment at 559 and 566 – 569.

Meadows v Khan

The Facts

In *Meadows v Khan*[45] the claimant brought a claim for damages based on wrongful birth, following the birth of a child with haemophilia. Prior to the conception of her child the claimant had consulted her doctor to establish whether she was a carrier for the haemophilia gene (her sibling having previously given birth to a child who suffered from haemophilia). Her doctor therefore arranged a blood test, but this only confirmed that the claimant herself did not have haemophilia and did not confirm whether or not she was a carrier, for which she would have needed a referral for genetic testing. She was however led to believe that the blood test had confirmed that she was not a carrier of the haemophilia gene and she subsequently fell pregnant.[46]

Her child unfortunately suffered from haemophilia and genetic testing later revealed that the claimant was in fact a carrier of the gene. Had she been aware of that during her pregnancy she would have undergone foetal testing, and had she learned her child suffered from haemophilia then she would have terminated the pregnancy.

The claimant's child also suffered from autism, unrelated to the haemophilia, and she claimed damages in relation to the extra costs associated with the autism, as well as those related to the haemophilia. It was undisputed that as a result of negligence the claimant was entitled to damages including the extra maintenance costs associated with her child's haemophilia. The key issue which the court was required to determine was the scope of the defendant's duty of care and whether it would be fair, just and reasonable to award damages for the extra maintenance costs which related to the child's autism in addition.

Yip J, delivering judgment, held that the legal issue she was required to determine was as follows[47]:

---

45 [2017] EWHC 2990 (Q.B.).

46 *Ibid.* at [1] and [5] – [7].

> *"Can a mother who consults a doctor with a view to avoiding the birth of a child with a particular disability (rather than to avoid the birth of any child) recover damages for the additional costs associated with an unrelated disability?"*

The claimant argued that she was entitled to damages for the continuation of the pregnancy and all of its consequences, including all disability related maintenance costs, in line with *Parkinson* in which the learning disability for which the claimant recovered damages was no more foreseeable than the child's autism here. The claimant argued that there could be no rational distinction drawn between a woman who did not want any pregnancy and one who did not want a particular pregnancy.[48]

In contrast the defendant argued that damages in respect of the child's autism fell outside the scope of the defendant's duty since the service the defendant had provided was only in relation to the risk of haemophilia. The defendant sought to distinguish between different types of wrongful birth cases and argued that there was a material distinction between the *"situation where a parent seeks to avoid the risk of a specific disability and one where the parent seeks to avoid or terminate the pregnancy"*: where a parent has sought to avoid any pregnancy there is no question of that parent having been willing to accept the usual risks of pregnancy that may lead to the birth of a disabled child, however where a parent has sought protection against a specific disability then they are otherwise happy to run the other usual risks associated with pregnancy.[49]

The Decision

Yip J began her judgment by finding there to be no basis on which to distinguish between wrongful birth and wrongful conception cases, finding so both *"as a matter of principle and having regard to the author-*

---

47 *Ibid.* at [2].

48 *Ibid.* at [1] and [47] – [49].

49 *Ibid.* at [1] and [50] – [51].

ities" and relying on *Groom v Selby*[50] as supporting authority.[51] She went further and held that wrongful birth arose either as a result of wrongful conception or because of negligence which denied the mother the opportunity to terminate a pregnancy: this case was unique in the sense that the negligence had occurred prior to conception.[52]

Yip J made the following findings:

- In respect of the scope of the defendant's duty[53]:
    - The focus of the duty was to provide the claimant with the necessary information to allow her to terminate any pregnancy affected by haemophilia.
    - The occurrence of autism was 'bad luck' but like the haemophilia it was a natural consequence of the pregnancy.[54]
    - The pregnancy in question would not have continued but for the negligence.
    - The scope of the defendant's duty extended to preventing this child's birth and all of the consequences of that birth.
    - The defendant did not assume any particular responsibility in relation to autism but did assume a responsibility

50 [2001] EWCA Civ 1522; also discussed in Chapter Six.

51 [2017] EWHC 2990 (Q.B.) at [8].

52 *Ibid.* at [9] – [10].

53 *Ibid.* at [62] – [63].

54 This is similar to the facts in *Groom v Selby* [2001] EWCA Civ 1522 where Hale LJ considered the occurrence of bacterium leading to salmonella meningitis and consequent brain injury was 'bad luck' but nonetheless compensable.

which *"if properly fulfilled, would have avoided the birth of the child in question,"* which was the same as had occurred in *Parkinson* and *Groom.*

- There was no difficulty with proximity or foreseeability: the child's autism was a congenital condition and a risk which existed for every pregnancy and it was a natural and foreseeable consequence of the birth.[55]

- Causation had been made out since the purpose of the service provided by the defendant was to prevent the claimant having a child with haemophilia. If that service had been performed properly then the defendant would have ensured that the pregnancy did not continue. The autism arose out of this pregnancy which would have been terminated but for the defendant's negligence and so but for the defendant's negligence the claimant's child would not have been born, and the claimant would not have to care for a child with the problems of haemophilia and autism.[56]

- She was not persuaded that the appropriate starting point was to consider the risks that a parent was willing to run, whether in this case where a parent did not want to have a child with a particular disability (and so would run the risks associated with pregnancy) or another type of case where the parent did not want any child (and so would not run any of the risks associated with pregnancy).[57] It was right that had the claimant known she was a carrier of the haemophilia gene then she still would have gone on to have another child (but would have simply undertaken foetal testing for haemophilia) and that pregnancy would also have carried a risk of autism. However, she held that on the

55 [2017] EWHC 2990 (Q.B.) at [22].

56 *Ibid.* at [26] and [53] – [58].

57 *Ibid.* at [52].

balance of probabilities that child would not have suffered from autism.[58]

- Addressing the recoverability of damages[59]:

    - The costs of raising a healthy child were not recoverable.

    - The extra costs of raising a disabled child were recoverable, even where there was no connection between the disability and the negligence, provided the disability arose out of the normal incidents of conception, intra-uterine development and birth, per *Groom* and *Parkinson*.[60]

    - The claimant was entitled to recover the extra maintenance costs associated with her child's autism.

    - The rising cost of professional indemnity for GPs was a matter of legitimate public concern but allowing recovery here would not open the floodgates since the co-existence of two disabilities would be rare.

    - The principles of distributive justice did not require a distinction to be drawn between the claimant who would have terminated her pregnancy in the instant case and a claimant who would have terminated any pregnancy.

    - The instant case ought to be decided by applying principles consistently with the way in which the Court of Appeal had applied them in previous wrongful birth

58 *Ibid.* at [37] – [46] and [54] – [55].

59 *Ibid.* at [11] – [20] and [64] – [70].

60 [2001] EWCA Civ 1522 and [2001] EWCA Civ 530; both discussed in Chapter Six.

> cases: it was *"unattractive to introduce further inconsistency by distinguishing different types of wrongful birth cases."*

Commentary

Meadows was decided on the basis that all wrongful birth and wrongful conception cases ought to be treated in the same manner. In part, Yip J relied on *Groom* in reaching that conclusion. However, in his judgment in *Groom* Brooke LJ appeared to distinguish between what he would call 'straightforward' wrongful birth cases where the negligence directly resulted in the birth of a disabled foetus and those like *Groom* where the disability which is the subject of a damages award has less of a direct link to the negligence (i.e. the same distinction as in *Meadows* between the haemophilia – which was the disability which the claimant had sought to avoid – and the autism – which was not connected to the negligence in the same way but was a natural consequence of the negligence having allowed the pregnancy to proceed). It does however seem that the facts in *Meadows* align with those in *Groom* and that the autism should be treated in much the same way that the meningitis was in *Groom.*

Regard must also be had to obiter remarks in *Rees* regarding the differing policy considerations which attach to wrongful birth cases, these obiter remarks being made without further explanation.[61] Although Brooke LJ provides some explanation in *Groom* regarding what those different considerations may be, it is not completely clear cut that wrongful birth and wrongful conception cases would be treated in the same way as each other by a superior court.

Yip J also acknowledges that the speeches in *Rees* cast some doubt on the reasoning of the Court of Appeal in *Parkinson* and *Groom,* in respect of awarding the extra maintenance costs associated with disability, but she still held that they were nonetheless binding on her (and she had not been asked to re-visit those decisions in any event).[62] Were

---

61 [2004] 1 A.C. 309; discussed in full in Chapter Seven.

62 [2017] EWHC 2990 (Q.B.) at [29].

the Supreme Court to re-visit *Parkinson* it is again by no means certain that the reasoning of the Court of Appeal would be upheld.[63]

Meadows appears to be the first reported case in which a different disability had arisen when the doctor had been consulted about another particular risk. In light of that and the uncertainties produced by previous Court of Appeal and House of Lords decisions it would not be surprising were this first instance decision in *Meadows* to face an appeal, though at present none has been confirmed.

Summary

There have been a number of recent cases which raise interesting questions about the limits of recovery in wrongful conception and wrongful birth cases. Recovery in such cases is already confined to allow only those additional maintenance costs incurred as a result of a child born with a disability, alongside the *Rees* conventional award. What is less clear are the limits of recovery if the father of a child were to bring a claim for those maintenance costs in his own right and the extent to which all wrongful conception and wrongful birth cases ought to be treated the same.

IVF Hammersmith concerned a father bringing a wrongful conception claim, though on the basis of contract. Interestingly, although there was discussion about the recoverability of damages in wrongful conception and wrongful birth claims when brought in negligence, the judgment did not touch on whether a father would have a stand-alone cause of action in those cases. This is perhaps understandable in the context of *IVF Hammersmith* which concerned the implantation of an embryo resulting in an unwanted child, as opposed to the failed prevention of a conception or birth where the position of the father is different. At the time of writing *IVF Hammersmith* is awaiting appeal and it remains to

---

63 See Chapter Six for a full discussion of *Parkinson*; see Chapter Seven for the judgments in *Rees;* see Chapter Thirteen for discussion regarding the future of wrongful conception and wrongful birth claims.

be seen how the Court of Appeal will approach the question of the recoverability of damages for maintenance costs in a contractual setting.

Whitehead is a case in which a father was asserting his right to bring a wrongful birth claim, though here in the context of a professional negligence action. *Whitehead* casts some doubt over whether a father in wrongful conception and wrongful birth claims would have a stand-alone cause of action. It is likely to be rare that a father would find himself in a position where he needs to bring a stand-alone claim, though as Rix LJ points out in *Whitehead* one can easily envisage a scenario where a mother dies in childbirth and therefore only the father can make such a claim (and there will doubtless be other scenarios in which it would be necessary, such as if the mother has absconded or is otherwise unable to claim for example). It does however appear that the law has been left open as to what would happen in these circumstances.

Finally, *Meadows* tests again the boundaries of the recoverability of damages in wrongful conception and wrongful birth cases with the *Parkinson* exception continuing to be utilised despite some judicial doubts as to the extent to which this remains good law (of course unless and until the issue is re-visited by a superior court lower courts will continue to be bound by it). It would certainly be interesting were *Meadows* to be heard on appeal, since this would represent a re-visiting of *Parkinson* for the first time in well over a decade.

In these controversial areas of law which have remained unchanged for some years it may well be time that they came before a superior court again.

CHAPTER TEN
QUANTUM

Damages Summary

As wrongful life is not presently a viable claim this chapter focuses on the damages available in wrongful conception and wrongful birth actions. As has been explored in previous chapters it has long been established that, in a wrongful conception or wrongful birth claim where the child is born healthy, maintenance costs are not a recoverable head of damages.

Notwithstanding the restrictions on damages in these types of cases there are still a number of recoverable heads of loss. A claim for damages in such cases will typically include:

- Any losses directly related to the pregnancy and childbirth:
    - General damages to reflect the pain, suffering and loss of amenity (PSLA) caused by an unwanted pregnancy and childbirth. The usual principles governing the assessment of PSLA will apply here (and see below for examples of the damages awarded).
    - Financial losses caused by the pregnancy and childbirth directly, such as maternity clothes, loss of earnings of the mother (where these are due to time off to recover etc. and not due to time off to look after the child) and medical expenses including treatment, equipment and medicines.
- The conventional award of £15,000.

All of the losses claimed will need to be properly evidenced, by both witness evidence and documentary evidence where possible.

For those cases where the child is born with a disability there will also need to be a careful calculation of the additional maintenance costs which arise as a result of the disability, over and above those maintenance costs which would be incurred in the event that a healthy child had been born. A damages claim for these extra maintenance costs can be expected to include:

- Medical treatment, including rehabilitative therapies.
- Aids and equipment.
- Care and assistance.
- Specialist care services.
- Case management costs.
- Additional travel costs, including for example the cost of an appropriate vehicle.
- Alterations to accommodation.
- Specialist or additional education.

Reported Damages Awards

There have been relatively few reported cases from which practitioners can take guidance as to the appropriate level of damages in these types of case:

- In *Meadows v Khan*[1] the damages award was £9,000,000 (including the extra maintenance costs associated with raising a child with both autism and haemophilia, where the child's autism complicated the care needs of the child in respect of the

1 [2017] EWHC 2990; discussed in full in Chapter Nine.

haemophilia). Had the court found that only the haemophilia was relevant for the assessment of damages then the award would have been £1,400,000.

- *FP v Taunton and Somerset NHS Trust*[2] was a wrongful birth case which twice came before the High Court on the issue of interim payments. The child in this case suffered from congenital disabilities and there was considerable uncertainty regarding his life expectancy. He relied on ventilation and required significant care as well as the provision of alternative accommodation. The total interim payments which were to be made, following an order for a further sum, was £2,200,000. This provides some indication of the amount of damages which the court considered it likely would be awarded at a final trial.[3]

- *XV v Mayday Healthcare NHS Trust*[4] was a wrongful birth claim brought following the birth of a disabled child. The claimant had notified her GP and midwives that she had concerns that there was a history of spinal muscular atrophy in her partner's family, but this was not followed up with a referral to a consultant or testing. It was later established that both the claimant and her partner were carriers for the condition and testing to check for the condition could have been carried out at 11 weeks of pregnancy. The claimant alleged that had she been told that there was a risk her child would be born with the condition then she would have terminated the pregnancy. The claimant claimed for her own psychiatric injury and the pain and suffering of pregnancy and labour. She also claimed for the care

2 [2009] EWHC 1965 (Q.B.) and [2011] EWHC 3380 (Q.B.).

3 Blair J in the first application ([2009] EWHC 1965 (Q.B.)) also considered whether there ought to be a stay and ordered that there be a further stay of two years (even though the child was already aged five) as the child's prognosis was unclear. It can be expected that many wrongful birth actions will face those same difficulties and stays would be common were the issue of a stay to be litigated.

4 (2012) Lawtel, Out of Court Settlement.

costs associated with her child's disability, who required 24-hour care, had a life expectancy of 16 to 17 years old and had significant physical disabilities though no cognitive impairment.

Liability was admitted and a total of £2,300,000 (c£2,604,357 RPI) was agreed, with the claimant's solicitor estimating the following breakdown of damages:

- PSLA: £35,000.
- Future care: £1,300,000.
- Future psychological therapy costs: £8,500.
- Future physiotherapy costs: £64,800.
- Future occupational therapy costs: £22,000.
- Future speech and language therapy costs: £20,000.
- Future aid and equipment costs: £86,000.
- Future assistive technology costs: £54,000.
- Future accommodation costs: £450,000.
- Future 'increased costs' (it is not clear what this relates to): £85,000.
- Future case management costs: £50,000.
- Past losses (towards gratuitous care, paid and gratuitous case management and miscellaneous expenses): £124,700.

- *T v Mayday Healthcare NHS Trust*[5] was a wrongful conception claim, brought following an allegedly negligent sterilisation operation which resulted in the conception and birth of a healthy baby. The claimant suffered from pre-existing lupus and the pregnancy made her symptoms worse.

  Liability was disputed. Nonetheless the matter was settled for a sum of £30,000 (£39,096 RPI), with the claimant's solicitor estimating the following breakdown of damages:

  - A *Rees* conventional award of £15,000.
  - PSLA (related to the pregnancy and childbirth as well as the exacerbation of lupus disease): £10,000.
  - Unspecified special damages: £5,000.

- *(1) EA v (2) AA v King's Lynn & Wisbech Hospitals NHS Trust*[6] was a wrongful birth claim brought following negligent screening for congenital disabilities, resulting in the birth of twins with severe Down's syndrome. The twins had a life expectancy of 60 years old but without capacity, the ability to live independently or prospects of employment. The twins exhibited challenging behaviour and required significant levels of care. The mother had suffered a moderately severe adjustment reaction and was at risk of further depressive illness and the father had suffered from a depressive episode which was ongoing at the time of settlement. The claimant alleged that screening appropriate for a multiple pregnancy ought to have been provided, and if it had resulted in a Down's syndrome diagnosis the claimant would have terminated her pregnancy.

  Liability was disputed but settlement was reached on the basis that damages would be assessed on a full liability basis and that

5 (2009) Lawtel, Out of Court Settlement.

6 (2007) Kemp & Kemp / Lawtel, Out of Court Settlement.

the defendant would pay 70% of those damages (to reflect litigation risk). Damages were agreed in the sum of £2,143,000 of which the defendant would pay 70%, so £1,500,00 (£2,005,529 RPI), which was broken down as £25,000 for PSLA and £1,475,000 for past and future losses (which amounts to c£35,714 and c£2,107,143 respectively if on a full liability basis).

- *U v Hammersmith Hospitals NHS Trust*[7] was a wrongful birth claim. The claimant gave birth to a child who was later diagnosed as suffering from a chromosomal abnormality; she alleged that the defendant had failed to detect the chromosomal abnormalities on an amniocentesis and had therefore failed to provide the claimant with the option of undergoing a termination. The claimant's child suffered from multiple different complex difficulties as a result of her chromosomal abnormalities which were both physical and developmental; she had a normal life expectancy of 65 years old but would require 24-hour care for her entire life.

  Liability was admitted. Damages were agreed on a global basis at £1,200,000 (£1,681,209 RPI) with an additional separate indemnity of £300,000 towards the child's education up to the age of 19 years old. The claimant's solicitors estimated that out of the total damages an appropriate award for general damages for the birth of a disabled child was in the region of £40,000.

- *C v East Cheshire NHS Trust*[8] was another wrongful birth claim in which the claimant alleged that the defendant had not carried out appropriate antenatal testing and had failed to diagnose a viral infection which caused the child to suffer from disabilities. The claimant alleged that had she been informed of this risk she would have terminated the pregnancy. The claimant also suffered from a mild to moderate depressive illness as a result of learning that her child was disabled.

7 (2006) Lawtel, Out of Court Settlement.

8 (2005) Lawtel, Out of Court Settlement.

Liability was partially admitted: the defendant argued that their liability in damages ceased upon the child reaching 18 years of age since that was also when the claimant's responsibility towards her child ceased and any care or accommodation needs after that date would be met by the local authority. The defendant also denied liability for the claimant's own psychiatric injury, arguing that this loss was too remote. Ultimately, damages were agreed on a global basis in the total sum of £2,500,000 (£3,581,917 RPI), which included the claimant's psychiatric injury and costs for the child's care past 18 years of age. The claimant's solicitor estimated the following breakdown of damages:

- PSLA: £25,000 (including £15,000 for the wrongful birth and £10,000 for psychiatric injury).
- Future losses (including the mother's loss of earnings, care and case management, travel, aid/equipment, education, accommodation, IT and therapies): £225,000.
- Future accommodation (which appears to have been double counted as accommodation is also included in the above category): £500,000.
- Future care and case management (which also appears in the generic future loss category already): £1,500,000.
- Past losses: £250,000.

• *(1) Heath (2) Heath (3) Heath v Bromley Health Authority*[9] concerned a claim brought by three children who suffered injuries as a result of having been born prematurely. There were also concurrent wrongful conception and wrongful birth claims. The parents were undergoing fertility treatment with the defendant, as a result of which the mother fell pregnant with quadruplets.

---

9 (2003) Lawtel, Out of Court Settlement.

She gave birth prematurely and the children suffered injury as a consequence. The claimants alleged that the defendant had been negligent in respect of the management, monitoring and administration of the fertility treatment and for a failure to refer the mother for appropriate advice regarding fetal reduction.

Liability was agreed by consent between the defendant and claimant children, which included deductions on the claimants' claims. Damages were agreed and approved in the sum of £2,008,500 (£3,080,882 RPI), split between three and after deductions (these were of course claims on behalf of the children themselves and so not strictly relevant to the quantum of damages for the parents' own claims, though do give an indication of the costs associated with the children's disabilities). What is interesting about this report is that it indicates that the defendant had also admitted liability for the parents' claim in respect of the failure to manage the fertility treatment appropriately, though no further particulars of negligence are provided; this provides some insight in to the way in which wrongful conception and wrongful birth actions in the context of fertility treatments might be responded to by defendants.

- *T v M*[10] concerned a failure by the defendant to timeously diagnose the claimant's pregnancy. As a consequence, the claimant gave birth to a child and brought an action for wrongful birth. It appears that the child was born healthy, though this is not explicitly stated in the report. The claimant was already the mother to two teenage children and had to give up her career to care for the new baby. She also had to undergo a planned caesarean operation due to the position of her baby.

  Liability was admitted and damages were agreed in the total sum of £22,500 (£34,099.46 RPI) broken down as:

  - A *Rees* conventional award: £15,000.

10 (2003) Lawtel, Out of Court Settlement.

- PSLA: £5,000.
- Special damages (including loss of earnings and baby layette): £2,500.

Any damages awards which relate to out of court settlements should obviously be treated with caution, since generally these awards are made on behalf of the adult claimant parent and are therefore not subject to court approval (and so have not been scrutinised by the court). Practitioners should also exercise caution where liability was disputed and / or the breakdown of damages has been provided by only one of the parties.

Commentary

The available reports on damages provide practitioners with an indication as to how these cases are likely to be valued. It appears that in most wrongful birth cases the heads of loss of highest value are likely to be the care costs and the accommodation costs; it should be remembered that these costs should only represent the extra maintenance costs associated with the disability, and so the care or accommodation needs of a healthy child ought to be stripped out of any damages award.

It should also be noted that some of the damages awards in respect of a disabled child appear not to account for the *Rees* conventional award of £15,000, even though it is expected that this award would apply to all cases whether the child is born healthy or disabled.[11]

The reports also provide interesting insight in to the way in which practitioners are dealing with some of the other issues for which there is not yet any clear resolution, as well as novel issues. The awards include a damages award for the father in a wrongful birth action, a claim for a multiple pregnancy,[12] a claim for the layette, and additional general damages claims for psychiatric injury suffered by the parents in such

11 As is explained in Chapter Seven.

actions. Some of these areas were discussed in Chapters Eight and Nine and they are further discussed in Chapter Thirteen.

12 This issue has been addressed by the Australian Courts in *G and M v Armellin* [2009] ACTA 6, discussed in full in Chapter Twelve.

CHAPTER ELEVEN
LESSONS FROM ABROAD: WRONGFUL LIFE

Introduction

At the time that *McKay v Essex Area Health Authority and Another*[1] was decided there was very limited useful authority from the United Kingdom or the Commonwealth. There was however a body of authority from the United States of America, which Stephenson LJ found to be persuasive authority in determining *McKay*.[2] Since the decision in *McKay* there have been a number of decisions in other jurisdictions which have confronted the issue of wrongful life.

A full examination of wrongful life claims in other jurisdictions is outside the scope of this book. This chapter aims to provide an overview of some of the decisions from abroad which have also had to confront wrongful life, both prior to and following the key decision in the United Kingdom, *McKay*. Although the pattern of such authority has tended towards denying wrongful life claims, with many courts relying on *McKay*, these cases still provide useful insight into the way in which this area of law is being dealt with across the globe.

United States of America

Gleitman v Cosgrove

Gleitman v Cosgrove was a decision of the Supreme Court of New Jersey in 1967.[3] In *Gleitman* the mother had been infected by German measles during pregnancy and as a result her son was born handicapped. It was alleged that the defendants had been negligent in failing to properly

---

1 [1982] Q.B. 1166; discussed in full in Chapter Three.

2 *Ibid.* at 1182 – 1184.

3 (1967) 227 A. 2d 689.

inform the mother of the effect such an infection would have on her unborn child. Each member of the family brought a claim: the child for his birth defects, the mother for the emotional consequences of having given birth to a disabled son, and the father for the maintenance costs occasioned by his son's birth. All of the claims were rejected. The child's case was rejected on the basis that his claim did not give rise to damages which were recognised by the law; it was not possible to calculate damages on the claim that was being made, which was that he would have been better off not having been born at all.[4]

Cases After Gleitman

Gleitman is the primary authority in rejecting wrongful life cases and has been followed by the vast majority of subsequent cases in the United States of America. These cases include the following:

- *Becker v Schwartz*[5]: The Appeals Court of New York rejected a claim brought by a child who had been born with Down's syndrome, on the basis that it disclosed no recognised cause of action and that it would depend on the comparison of life in an impaired state with non-existence, which was *"a comparison the law is not equipped to make."*[6]

- *Park v Chessin*[7]: The Appeals Court of New York also rejected a claim brought by a child who had been born suffering from polycystic kidney disease, on the same basis as *Becker* above.

- *Phillips v United States of America*[8]: The South Carolina District Court rejected another claim by a child born with Down's syndrome. The case was rejected even though it was found that the

4 *Ibid.* at 692 – 711.

5 (1978) 413 N.Y.S. 2d 895.

6 *Ibid.* at 900 – 903.

7 (1977) 60 A.D. 2d 80.

8 (1980) 508 F.Supp 537.

difficulty calculating damages and the fact that the negligence had not caused the defect were not bars to the claim. It was held that were the South Carolina Supreme Court asked to determine the matter it would reject the claim on the basis of public policy.[9]

- *Berman v Allan*[10]: The Supreme Court of New Jersey also rejected another claim by a child born with Down's syndrome, on the basis that the child had not suffered any damage cognizable at law by being brought into existence.[11]

- *Speck v Finegold*[12]: The Supreme Court of Pennsylvania rejected a claim brought by a child with a genetic disorder, finding that the child did not have a cause of action against the defendant physicians.

The case of *Curlender v Bio-Science Laboratories* did however permit an action for wrongful life.[13] In this case the defendant had negligently failed to detect that the child was suffering from Tay-Sachs disease via pre-natal testing. The Court of Appeal of California held that it was consistent with tort law to permit the child's wrongful life claim; since a duty existed which had been breached and had resulted in injury this was sufficient to establish a cause of action for the child.[14]

The judgment of Stephenson LJ in *McKay* provides a helpful summary of the principles which can be distilled from case law in the United States of America. The vast majority of the case law prior to *McKay*

---

9 *Ibid.* at 542 – 544.

10 (1979) 80 N.J. 421.

11 *Ibid.* at 428 – 429.

12 (1981) 497 Pa. 77.

13 (1980) App., 165 Cal.Rptr. 477.

14 *Ibid.* at 488 – 490.

found that wrongful life claims were not a valid cause of action on the following bases:[15]

- The real cause of action in wrongful life claims is that there has been negligence which has resulted in life.
- Negligent advice or a failure to advise is the cause of the child's life (though not of the child's disability).
- A child has no right to be born free from disability.
- Public policy includes the preservation of human life and it would be contrary to that aim to permit a child to have a right to be born free from disability (as this would necessarily entail the existence of a duty to cause the death of an unborn child with disabilities).
- It is impossible to compare existence with non-existence and so the calculation of damages is impossible.

Cases After McKay

Since *McKay*, *Curlender* has been overruled in part by the Supreme Court of California in *Turpin v Sortini,*[16] which held that general damages could not be awarded because of the impossibility in assessment which required a comparison between existence and non-existence. Special damages were however still awarded on the basis that these were *"both certain and readily measurable."*[17] *Curlender* was therefore overruled in part but affirmed in part in the same judgment.[18]

---

15 [1982] Q.B. 1166 at 1183 – 1184.

16 82 Cal Rptr 337 (1982).

17 *Ibid.* at 348.

18 The approach of the Supreme Court of California in *Turpin* was then very quickly followed by similar judgments by the Supreme Court of New Jersey in *Procanik v Cillo* 478 A 2d 755 (1984) and by the Supreme Court of Washington

More recently the Supreme Court of Oregon rejected a claim for wrongful life, in *Tomlinson v Metropolitan Paediatrics, LLC*[19]. A child was born with a genetic neuromuscular disorder, with which his older brother also suffered. It was alleged that the defendants had been negligent in failing to diagnose his older brother and inform his parents of the risks were they to have another child. His claim was rejected on the basis that a claim by the child involved the impossible comparison between existence and non-existence. It was also held that there was *"too much gap in settled principles of negligence law to bridge"* for the court to recognise the claim and accordingly there was no cognizable cause of action.[20]

Australia

Harriton v Stephens[21] is a decision of the High Court of Australia which addressed whether a wrongful life claim was actionable.[22] *Harriton* presented very similar facts to *McKay*: the claimant alleged that the defendant had been negligent in advising her mother that she had not suffered from rubella during pregnancy. In fact, the claimant's mother had contracted rubella and as a result the claimant suffered from congenital disabilities. It was agreed that just the claimant's mother had received negligent advice and had she been properly informed she would have terminated her pregnancy.

The High Court of Australia was required to determine whether or not wrongful life actions were permissible in law. The claim was dismissed,

---

in *Harbeson v Parke-Davis Inc* 656 P 2d 483 (1983).

19 (2018) 362 Or. 431.

20 *Ibid.* at 465 – 472.

21 [2006] HCA 15.

22 Prior to *Harriton* there had been other wrongful life claims brought in Australia which had been dismissed. See for example *Bannerman v Mills* (1991) Aust Tort Reports 81-079; *Hayne v Nyst* Unreported, Supreme Court of Queensland, 17 October 1995; *Edwards v Blomeley* [2002] NSWSC 460.

and wrongful life claims found not to be actionable, on the following basis[23]:

- The claimant was required to prove that she was owed a duty of care by the defendant doctor to avoid the damage of which she was complaining.
- She was therefore required to prove that she had suffered loss or damage. In order to do so she was required to show that she had suffered interference with a protected right or interest.
- The damage the claimant complained of was that she had been born into a life with disabilities. She was therefore claiming that the doctor's negligence had interfered with her right not to exist.
- Assessing this damage entailed an impossible comparison between existence with a disability and non-existence.
- It was *"odious and repugnant to devalue the life of a disabled person"* by permitting the claimant to assert that she would have been better off never having been born.
- As the alleged damage was not capable of legal recognition then there could not be a duty of care to avoid it.

Some interesting commentary can be found within Kirby J's dissenting judgment in *Harriton*. In particular he provides insight into the difficulty which can present itself in describing such claims as claims for 'wrongful life.' His view was that the term ought to be avoided for the following reasons[24]:

---

23 [2006] HCA 15 (Crennan J delivering the lead judgment) at [218] - [219], [225] and [242] – [278].

24 [2006] HCA 15 at [9] – [15].

- The historical origins of the phrase were not consistent with its modern use.

- To describe the claim as one for 'wrongful life' was *"seriously misleading"* since the claimant in such cases is not complaining about having been born but rather is pointing to the defendant's conduct as a wrong, as a result of which his life is disadvantaged.

- Using 'wrongful life' as a blanket term for all cases brought by children who would not have existed but for a defendant's negligence risked obscuring important factual distinctions which exist within cases of this type. There was also a risk that the similarities of these types of claim with wrongful birth actions brought by parents might be overlooked.

- The words 'wrongful life' *"denigrate the value of human existence"*, which might be a bar to dispassionate legal analysis of these types of claim.

Kirby J also draws attention to the flaws in the argument that wrongful life claims are doomed to fail because of the impossibility in calculating damages awards where this requires the comparison between existence and non-existence: he points to other legal scenarios where the courts engage in just such an exercise.[25]

The case of *Waller v James*[26] was heard at the same time as *Harriton.* That case involved an allegation of negligent genetic pre-natal testing which resulted in the birth of a child suffering from a hereditary disease. The child brought a claim for wrongful life, which was dismissed on the same basis as in *Harriton.*

---

25 *Ibid.* at [95].

26 [2006] HCA 16.

Canada

There have been relatively few wrongful life actions in Canada and those that are brought appear to be swiftly dismissed, with reliance placed on *McKay* by the courts:

- *Arndt v Smith*[27]: A wrongful life claim brought following the contraction by the mother of chicken pox during pregnancy was dismissed.

- *Jones (Guardian ad Loren of) v Rostvig*[28]: A wrongful life claim brought following the birth of a child with Down's syndrome, after a negligent failure to advise testing for the same, was dismissed.

- *Hergott v Bovingdon*[29]: A fairly recent wrongful life claim was dismissed where the mother had been provided with a fertility drug which resulted in the conception of twins, and the twin pregnancy caused premature birth, which in turn resulted in both twins suffering from disabilities.

Singapore

The courts of Singapore have also rejected wrongful life claims. In *JU v See Tho Kai Yin*[30] a child born with Down's syndrome brought a wrongful life action alleging that the defendant was negligent in failing to warn his mother of the risk of her child suffering from chromosomal abnormalities and failing to advise her of the available tests for the same. His case was dismissed on the basis that there was no valid cause of action and again *McKay* was relied upon.[31]

---

27 (1994) 93 BCLR (2d) 220.

28 (1999) 44 CCLT (2d) 313

29 (2008) ONCA 2.

30 [2005] 4 SLR 96.

Summary

The progression of authority in other jurisdictions demonstrates a similar approach to that taken in the United Kingdom, which is to reject wrongful life claims by holding that they do not disclose a valid cause of action.

Recent judgments from abroad demonstrate the potential areas for development of the law, as different areas of negligence arise alongside medical advancements. Some authority also provides interesting insight into alternative approaches which could be taken when addressing wrongful life claims: in particular Kirby J's dissent in *Harriton v Stephens* provides a different viewpoint on this type of case.

Chapter Twelve explores the approach of foreign jurisdictions to wrongful conception and wrongful birth claims. Chapter Thirteen explores the current legal position and the lessons that can be learned from the treatment of wrongful life cases both in England and abroad, and whether or not the law in relation to those claims is ever likely to change.

---

31 *Ibid.* at [95] – [99].

CHAPTER TWELVE
LESSONS FROM ABROAD: WRONGFUL CONCEPTION AND WRONGFUL BIRTH

Introduction

When *McFarlane v Tayside Health Board*[1] addressed the recoverability of maintenance costs in wrongful conception and wrongful birth cases guidance was taken from other jurisdictions. Prior to *McFarlane* there was a pattern tending towards permitting the recovery of maintenance costs in the United Kingdom different approaches were taken in other jurisdictions.

A full examination of the way in which these claims have been dealt with by foreign jurisdictions is outside of the scope of this book. This chapter provides an overview of the decisions from foreign jurisdictions which informed the judgments in the key cases in the United Kingdom, as well as exploring those recent decisions from foreign jurisdictions which confront some of the remaining unanswered questions in this area of law and provide potential areas for development of the law in the United Kingdom.

United States of America

The United States of America presents a spectrum of decisions with some courts denying recovery altogether and other courts awarding generous damages. Some examples are as follows:

- *Szekeres v Robinson*[2]: The Supreme Court of Nevada rejected a claim for damages. The court held that the birth of a healthy albeit unwanted child did not present damage for which com-

1 [2000] 2 A.C. 59; discussed in full in Chapter Five.

2 (1986) 715 P.2d 1076.

pensation ought to be provided as *"normal birth is not a wrong, it is a 'right.' It ... is not a legally compensable injurious consequence"* regardless of whether it was attributable to the negligence.[3]

- *Lovelace Medical Center v Mendez*[4]: The Supreme Court of New Mexico recognised that a failed sterilisation invaded the claimants' financial security (where the sterilisation had been undertaken to conserve resources) and that this amounted to a compensable injury.[5] Damages were awarded for maintenance costs and for the pain and suffering associated with pregnancy and birth. The court also held that the emotional benefits that a child brought could not be offset from the financial detriment suffered by the claimants, since this would not be offsetting like-for-like.[6]

- *Johnson v University Hospitals of Cleveland*[7]: The Supreme Court of Ohio held that the parents were only entitled to damages for the cost of the pregnancy itself and the maintenance costs of the child were excluded. The judgment appears to be based on public policy concerns against classifying the birth of a normal, healthy child as an injury.[8]

- *Smith v Cote*[9]: The Supreme Court of New Hampshire recognised a claim for wrongful birth, holding that the damages ought to include the extraordinary medical and educational costs as well as costs associated with extraordinary parental care,

---

3 *Ibid.* at 1078 – 1079.

4 (1991) 805 P.2d 603.

5 *Ibid.* at 612.

6 *Ibid.* at 613.

7 (1989) 540 N.E.2d 1370.

8 *Ibid.* at 1378.

9 (1986) 128 H.H. 231.

as a result of raising the impaired child. Restricting damages to the extraordinary costs associated with the child's impairment was appropriate to establish a *"necessary and clearly defined boundary to liability in this area."*[10]

- *McKernan v Aasheim*[11]: The Supreme Court of Washington rejected a claim for damages for maintenance costs. The court held that it was not possible to establish that the birth of a healthy child amounted to damage suffered by its parents and to permit recovery would be contrary to public policy.[12]

- *Zehr v Jaugen*[13]: The Supreme Court of Oregon held that claimants were entitled to include a claim for maintenance costs in their pleadings (such a claim being brought in contract and negligence). It was held that these costs, which also included the expense of college education, were not so speculative as to be irrecoverable.[14]

- *Public Health Trust v Brown*[15]: A claim for maintenance costs following a negligent sterilisation was refused by the Supreme Court of Florida, on the basis that the birth and rearing of a healthy child did not amount to damage. It was held that the benefits of parenthood outweighed the monetary burdens imposed on the claimants, which was evidenced by the fact that the parents did not elect for abortion or adoption services in respect of their child.[16]

---

10 *Ibid.* at 344 – 351.

11 (1984) 687 P.2d 850.

12 *Ibid.* at 851 - 856.

13 (1994) 318 Or. 647.

14 *Ibid.* at 651 - 657.

15 (1980) 388 So.2d 1048.

16 *Ibid.* at 1085 – 1086.

- *Chaffee v Seslar*[17]: The Supreme Court of Indiana held that in a wrongful conception claim, following an allegedly negligent sterilisation, the recoverable damages could not include the costs of raising and educating a normal, healthy child since the benefits of the child's life outweighed any financial burdens occasioned by it.[18]

- *Sherlock v Stillwater Clinic*[19]: The Supreme Court of Minnesota awarded some damages, having calculated as closely as was possible an appropriate reduction on the damages to reflect the non-financial benefits which are brought by the birth of a child.[20] It was not considered that the failure of the claimants to utilise adoption or abortion services amounted to a failure to mitigate damages. Maintenance costs for a healthy child were also not ordinarily expected to extend past the child's age of majority, since this was when the parental duty to support the child ceased (though the situation might be different in cases concerning disabled children).[21]

Some of the cases in which wrongful life was considered[22] also held that a wrongful birth action by the parents would succeed and addressed the extent to which damages would be recoverable: in *Berman v Allan*[23] and

---

17 (2003) 786 N.E. 2d 705.

18 *Ibid.* at 706 – 709.

19 (1977) 260 N.W.2d 169.

20 *Sherlock v Stillwater Clinic* was cited in the English cases of *Thake v Maurice* [1986] Q.B. 644 and *Allan v Greater Glasgow Health Board* 1998 S.L.T. 580 but received some criticism in *McFarlane v Tayside Health Board* [2000] 2 A.C. 59 at 92 – 93.

21 (1977) 260 N.W.2d 169 at 174 – 177.

22 Discussed in full in Chapter Eleven.

23 (1979) 80 N.J. 421 at 431 – 434.

Park v Chessin[24] no maintenance costs were awarded, but in *Speck v Finegold*[25] maintenance costs were awarded.

In *Parkinson v St James and Seacroft University Hospital NHS Trust*[26] Brooke LJ found that the cases from the United States of America were of no assistance in wrongful conception or wrongful birth claims where a disabled child had been born since those cases tended to deny damages on the basis of reasonable foreseeability and the English law was developing in that regard. The House of Lords in *Rees v Darlington Memorial Hospital NHS Trust*[27] did not consider in any great detail the position in other jurisdictions, the House of Lords in *McFarlane* having already undertaken a review of the applicable case law.

In a recent wrongful birth case, *Plowman v Fort Madison Community Hospital*,[28] the Supreme Court of Iowa upheld a claim for wrongful birth on an appeal of a summary judgment application. The court specifically held that it appeared that the father was entitled to bring a wrongful birth claim notwithstanding that he was not himself a patient of the defendant; fathers in such cases had a *"voice in reproductive decisions,"* it was *"particularly compelling"* that the father had a joint legal obligation to support the child and it was easily foreseeable that harm would result to both parents (not just the mother) in these cases.[29]

Doe 1 v Xytex Corporation[30] is another recent wrongful birth case concerning the provision of sperm via a sperm donation service, where the claimants alleged that the sperm which they had been provided was 'defective and unsafe', following their discovery that the sperm donor (contrary to representations made by the defendant) was a schizo-

24 (1977) 60 A.D. 2d 80 at 94 – 119.

25 (1981) 497 Pa. 77 at 90 – 118.

26 [2001] EWCA Civ 530, [2002] Q.B. 266; discussed in full in Chapter Six.

27 [2004] 1 A.C. 309; discussed in full in Chapter Seven.

28 (2017) 896 N.W.2d 393.

29 *Ibid.* at 411 – 413.

30 (2017) WL 1112996.

phrenic criminal. The claim for product liability under negligence was upheld by the United States District Court, N.D. California, on the defendant's motion to dismiss, and the case was to proceed to trial. This is an example of the newer types of wrongful conception and wrongful birth claims that are likely to be seen with advancements in medical technologies.

Australia

C.E.S. Superclinics (Australia) Pty. Ltd[31] is a wrongful birth claim, decided in Australia prior to the lead case of *Cattanach v Melchior,*[32] and which received judicial attention in *McFarlane.*[33]

There was split opinion in the Court of Appeal in *CES*: Meagher JA would have denied the entirety of the claim on a public policy basis, Priestly JA would have allowed the claim but would have excluded maintenance costs, and Kirby A.C-J would have allowed the claim, including maintenance costs, provided that any benefits were offset (although he ultimately agreed with Priestly JA to ensure a majority decision was reached, which was to permit damages associated with pregnancy and childbirth but to deny damages for maintenance costs).

By the time that the English House of Lords heard *Rees,* the case of *Cattanach v Melchior*[34] had been heard by the High Court of Australia. The claim in *Cattanach* arose out of an allegedly negligent sterilisation (following which a normal, healthy child was born) and the High Court was asked to determine the recoverability of damages for the maintenance costs of the child.[35] The High Court, by a narrow majority (4:3) allowed the appeal and awarded damages for maintenance costs on

31 (1995) 38 N.S.W.L.R. 47.

32 [2003] HCA 38, discussed below.

33 [2000] 2 A.C. 59 at 112; discussed in full in Chapter Five.

34 [2003] HCA 38.

35 *Ibid.*

the basis that recovery was within the ordinary application of tortious principles and was not precluded by policy considerations. Kirby J and Callinan J addressed *McFarlane*, finding there to be disparity of reasoning between their Lordships and finding that ultimately the decision in *McFarlane* was reached on the basis of public policy considerations. The majority in *Cattanach* rejected the following arguments against recovery of maintenance costs:

- That permitting such a claim negatively affected the value of the life of the child in question: the damage which was complained of was simply the financial burden arising from the birth of the child.[36]

- That the birth of a child was always a blessing: this was not always the case and should only be stated if supported on the evidence in a particular case.[37]

- That an award of damages would be detrimental to the child, upon learning that they were unwanted: this was too speculative.[38]

- That there should be an offset for the intangible benefits of parenthood: the benefits and burdens in question were part of separate legal interests which should not be compared.[39]

The minority would have dismissed the claim for maintenance costs, relying on those policy considerations previously raised in cases such as *McFarlane* and also because of considerations of the importance attached to parenthood and concerns regarding the commodification of the life of the child.[40]

---

36 *Ibid.* at [67] – [68] and [146] – [148].

37 *Ibid.* at [79] – [83] and [148].

38 *Ibid.* at [79] and [301].

39 *Ibid.* at [84] – [90], [167] – [175] and [297] – [298].

40 *Ibid.* at [21] – [40], [182] – [263] and [304] – [412].

Following *Cattanach* the Australian Capital Territory Court of Appeal also addressed a wrongful conception case, this time in the context of IVF treatment, in *G v Armellin.*[41] The claimants in *Armellin* were undergoing IVF treatment under the care of the defendant. They wished to avoid a multiple pregnancy and so only wanted to undergo the implantation of one embryo; they alleged that the defendant had negligently implanted two embryos, which had resulted in the conception and birth of twins. The claimants brought a claim for wrongful conception on the basis that they had only ever wanted one child, and they claimed for damages to include the maintenance costs of the second additional child that had resulted from the negligent IVF treatment.

Although in the lower court the defendant escaped liability on the facts, the court finding that he had not breached a duty of care, he was subsequently held liable on appeal. In respect of the scope and extent of the duty of care the lower court did find that, notwithstanding the fact that it is not possible to choose whether to have a multiple pregnancy during natural reproduction, where this was a choice which was available and offered in assisted reproductive services then the claimant had a right to so choose.[42]

It was also held that this type of case was still a valid wrongful conception case, notwithstanding that the claimants had undergone the treatment because they specifically wanted a child, since the second, 'additional' child was still an unwanted child and there had thus been the creation of a parent-child relationship against the claimants' wishes.[43] Interestingly however, the judgment made specific reference to *Cattanach* and would have favoured the decision of the minority, were that judgment not binding.[44]

---

41 [2009] ACTCA 6; see also the earlier decision of the Supreme Court at [2008] ACTSC 68.

42 [2008] ACTSC 68 at [70].

43 *Ibid.* at [129] – [154].

44 *Ibid.* at [2].

Ultimately, following *Cattanach,* legislation was introduced in three Australian States which placed restrictions on the damages that can be claimed in wrongful conception and wrongful birth claims in these States, effectively reversing the outcome of *Cattanach*.

Canada

In *Kealey v Berezowski*[45] maintenance costs were not awarded. Lax J, delivering judgment, held that *"as a matter of public policy, the financial responsibilities associated with the care and upbringing of a child are the responsibilities of the parents."*[46]

Since *Kealey* there appears to have been somewhat of a shift in the Canadian approach particularly in British Columbia. Two cases which came after *Rees* was decided appeared to adopt the approach taken in *Rees*, to award damages akin to the conventional sum awarded there:

- *Bevilacqua v Altenkirk*[47]: A wrongful conception claim was brought by both parents, following the negligent communication of test results post-vasectomy which resulted in the conception and birth of a normal, healthy child.

- *Roe v Dabbs*[48]: A wrongful birth claim was brought following a negligent abortion which resulted in the birth of a child.

In both cases damages were awarded which comprised what the courts described as non-pecuniary in nature; in *Bevilacqua* this award was made to both the mother and the father.

---

45 (1996) 136 D.L.R. (4th) 708 at 739 – 741.

46 *Ibid.* at 739.

47 [2004] B.C.S.C. 945.

48 [2005] B.C.S.C. 957.

Singapore

The recent case of *ACB v Thomson Medical Pte Ltd and Others*[49] was a wrongful birth case arising out of IVF treatment. The parents brought a claim following the birth of their second child, conceived via IVF, when they noticed that she did not resemble them as their first child had done: genetic testing later confirmed that the child was only related to the mother as an anonymous donor's sperm had been used instead of the mother's husband's sperm. The parents brought a claim for wrongful birth and sought damages to include maintenance costs for the child.[50]

An interesting aspect of this case is that the court considered that the claim did not really fit into any of the usual categories in this area of law: not wrongful life (because the claimant was the parent), not wrongful birth (because the mother did not claim she would have terminated the pregnancy) and not wrongful conception (because the mother wanted to conceive a child, but a child with her husband's DNA and not with the DNA of the anonymous donor). The court considered that this case was properly categorised as a wrongful fertilisation claim.[51] The court also considered that focussing solely on the financial aspect of the wrong by way of assessment of maintenance costs was *"as a statement of parenthood, strikingly inadequate."* As such, whether punitive damages or an award for loss of autonomy ought to be awarded was also considered; ultimately the court decided against both of these types of award (with an award for loss of autonomy found to be too nebulous a concept, outside of the remit of usual tortious principles and likely to undermine the existing control mechanisms for damages in tort).[52]

The Supreme Court upheld the claim but did not make an award of damages for maintenance costs, on the basis that this was contrary to

49 [2017] SGCA 20.

50 *Ibid.* at [6] – [13].

51 *Ibid.* at [28] – [43].

52 *Ibid.* at [17] – [18], [106] – [124] and [153] – [209].

public policy as the obligation to maintain a child was *"at the heart of parenthood and cannot be a legally cognisable head of loss"* and to recognise such a claim would be inconsistent with the parent-child relationship.[53] The court also held that the outcome was the same whether the claim was brought in contract, or tort, since the policy considerations speaking against recovery were the same regardless of the cause of action.[54]

Of particular note is the finding that notwithstanding the rejection of this head of loss, damages ought to be awarded for a new head of loss, that of 'genetic affinity', which arose from considerations regarding the loss of autonomy present in these types of cases. The damages award for this new head of loss was made in the form of a conventional sum, which was actually calculated as a percentage of what the maintenance costs would have been in any event. The court however reserved the position on whether these types of damages awards would be appropriate in cases of wrongful conception and wrongful birth, as opposed to wrongful fertilisation.[55]

Summary

The way in which other jurisdictions have dealt with wrongful conception and wrongful birth claims provide insight into the spectrum of legal opinion in these areas across the globe. The more recent cases also demonstrate the way in which the law is required to adapt and respond

53 *Ibid.* at [24] and [86] – [100].

54 *Ibid.* at [54] and [102] – [105].

55 *Ibid.* at [125] – [152]. Contrast the whole of the decision in *ACB* with similar decisions in the United States of America and the United Kingdom. In *Andrews v Keltz* (2007) 15 Misc.3d 940 the Supreme Court of New York addressed a claim by parents and a child, following the use of sperm from someone other than the intended father. In *A v A Health and Social Services Trust* [2011] NICA 28 the Court of Appeal of Northern Ireland held that children, born through IVF but with a different skin colour to that of their parents, had not suffered damage sufficient for the purposes of a negligence claim.

to medical advancements which present new factual matrices which do not necessarily fit within the established legal principles.

The Australian case of *Cattanach* is perhaps of most interest since the High Court there elected to depart from *McFarlane*. It is however worth noting that the legislative climate in Australia tends against permitting large damages awards in these types of claim. Shortly after *Cattanach*, legislation was introduced in some Australian states which reduced or removed the ability for claimants to bring such claims for damages in negligence.[56] As Kirby J noted in *Harriton v Stephens* the *"chief stated purpose of such legislation has been to reduce the cost of insurance premiums."*[57] Even were there to be a change in English law[58] then there would of course remain the risk that parliamentary intervention would operate to claw back any expanded entitlement to damages which was afforded to claimants.

Chapter Thirteen explores the current legal position, the lessons that can be learned from the treatment of wrongful conception, wrongful birth and wrongful life cases both in England and abroad, and whether or not the law in relation to those claims is ever likely to change.

56 See for example Section 70 and Section 71 of the *Civil Liability Act 2002 (NSW)* which places restrictions on wrongful birth claims brought in New South Wales.

57 [2006] HCA 15 at [134].

58 Which is discussed in more detail in Chapter Thirteen.

CHAPTER THIRTEEN
CONCLUSIONS: IS IT TIME FOR A RE-THINK?

Summary of the Law

Current Legal Position

As has been explored in the previous chapters, the following principles can be distilled from the progression of case law:

- Wrongful life claims are not presently recognised as a viable claim, per *McKay v Essex Area Health Authority and Another.*[1]
- The facts of wrongful life claims will often be indistinguishable from the facts of a wrongful birth claim, with the only substantive difference being that the claimants in the latter will be the parents of the child.
- A child is able to claim under the *Congenital Disabilities (Civil Liability) Act 1976* for disabilities caused by negligence, but these claims are different to claims for wrongful life.
- It appears that wrongful birth and wrongful conception claims will be treated the same when damages are being assessed, per *Meadows v Khan*[2] and *Groom v Selby*[3].
- No award of damages will be made for the maintenance costs of a healthy child, per *McFarlane v Tayside Health Board.*[4]

---

1 [1982] 2 Q.B. 1166; discussed in full in Chapter Three.

2 [2017] EWHC 2990; discussed in full in Chapter Nine.

3 [2001] EWCA Civ 1522; discussed in Chapter Six and Chapter Nine.

4 [2000] 2 A.C. 59; discussed in full in Chapter Five.

- There will also be no award of damages made where the loss of earnings of the parents is claimed in lieu of maintenance costs, per *Greenfield v Irwin*.[5]

- If a child is born with a disability then a damages award will be made which includes the extra maintenance costs associated with that disability, per *Parkinson v St James and Seacroft University Hospital NHS Trust*.[6]

- Whether or not a child has been born sufficiently disabled for the purposes of a damages award will be determined on a case-by-case basis, per *Parkinson v St James and Seacroft University Hospital NHS Trust*.

- All disabilities which are a 'natural and foreseeable consequence of childbirth' will result in a damages award being made for the extra maintenance costs associated with disability, even where the disability arises after childbirth or where the disability suffered is different to that which a mother initially sought to avoid, per *Meadows v Khan* and *Groom v Selby*.

- Where the parent of the child is disabled no additional damages associated with the parent's disability will be recoverable, per *Rees v Darlington Memorial Hospital NHS Trust*.[7]

- A conventional award of £15,000 will be awarded to claimants in wrongful birth and wrongful conception claims, per *Rees v Darlington Memorial Hospital NHS Trust*.

- Maintenance costs for a healthy child will be irrecoverable whether the claim is brought in contract or in tort, per *ARB v IVF Hammersmith and R*.[8]

---

5 [2001] EWCA Civ 113.

6 [2001] EWCA Civ 530; discussed in full in Chapter Six.

7 [2004] 1 A.C. 309; discussed in full in Chapter Seven.

- A claim for damages arising out of wrongful conception or wrongful birth amounts to damages in respect of personal injury for the purposes of the *Limitation Act 1980* and that one limitation period will apply across all of the heads of damage (including any claim for maintenance costs, which do not amount to a separate claim for pure economic loss but arise out of the same cause of action as the other heads of loss), per *Walkin v South Manchester Health Authority*.[9]

- Anonymity orders are likely to be granted in wrongful conception and wrongful birth cases.[10]

Of course, the more recent decisions are, or have the potential to be, subject to an appeal and there do remain some questions which have not yet been answered by the Supreme Court. Were a wrongful conception, wrongful birth or wrongful life case to come before the Supreme Court there may be a change to the above principles and at the very least it would be expected that the law governing the scope and extent of the recovery of damages in such cases would be refined further.

Remaining Uncertainty

Questions do however remain regarding the scope and application of the principles set out above, in particular:

- The extent to which *Parkinson* remains good law following some negative judicial comment in *Rees*.[11] It is not certain that

8 [2017] EWHC 2438 (Q.B.); discussed in full in Chapter Nine.

9 [1995] 1 WLR 1543; discussed in full in Chapter Four.

10 See for example *ARB v IVF Hammersmith and R* [2017] EWHC 2438 (Q.B.); *A v East Kent Hospitals University NHS Foundation Trust* [2015] EWHC 1038 (Q.B.); *XXX v King's College Hospital NHS Foundation Trust* [2018] EWHC 646 (Q.B.).

11 See further discussion in Chapter Seven.

Parkinson would be affirmed were the same issues to come before the Supreme Court, though lower courts have indicated that they are bound by the principles set out in *Parkinson* until such time as the Supreme Court re-visits them.[12]

- Whether wrongful conception and wrongful birth cases will be treated the same:

    - Although *Meadows v Khan*[13] and *Groom v Selby*[14] suggest that wrongful conception and wrongful birth cases are on the same footing it is to be noted that there is no express finding by the Supreme Court to this effect.

    - There are instead obiter remarks in *McFarlane, Parkinson* and *Rees* which suggest that different policy considerations apply across the two types of case.

    - In *Parkinson* Brooke LJ also made such obiter remarks. He did however seek to clarify what he had meant by these in the later case of *Groom v Selby*: there he appeared to assert that wrongful birth cases were more straightforward cases than wrongful conception and that is all he had meant when referencing different policy considerations.

    - Brooke LJ in *Groom v Selby* did also appear to distinguish between different types of wrongful birth claims, finding the facts of *Groom v Selby* to warrant closer examination than the usual run of wrongful birth cases. This suggests that even within wrongful birth claims there still needs to be a thorough analysis of the facts

12 See for example *Meadows v Khan* [2017] EWHC 2990 at [29], discussed in full in Chapter Nine, and *FP v Taunton and Somerset NHS Trust,* [2009] EWHC 1965 at [7].

13 [2017] EWHC 2990; discussed in full in Chapter Nine.

14 [2001] EWCA Civ 1522; discussed in Chapter Six and Chapter Nine.

and basis for the claim, rather than simply applying the same principles across the board.

- The extent to which a father would have a stand-alone cause of action:

    - In many of the previous wrongful conception cases claims have been brought by both parents as claimants and there has been no challenge to the status of the father as claimant.

    - *Whitehead v Searle*[15] cast some doubt over whether a father would be able to bring a stand-alone wrongful conception or wrongful birth claim, suggesting that this had yet to be determined. Certainly fathers in such cases would first have to establish that they were owed a duty of care[16] and even then they may face more difficult evidential hurdles since they may not necessarily be able to lead evidence from the mother as to her intentions regarding pregnancy (the mother may have died, like in *Whitehead v Searle*, or have absconded for example, but the father will still have to establish that but for the negligence the child would not have been born[17]).

---

15 [2008] EWCA Civ 285, [2009] 1 W.L.R. 549;, also known as *McLeish (Deceased), Re Hibbert Pownall & Newton (A Firm) v Whitehead*; discussed in Chapter Nine

16 See for example *Goodwill v British Pregnancy Advisory Service* [1996] 1 WLR 1397, also discussed in Chapter Two. A father would be in an even more tenuous position than the mother was in *Goodwill*, having also sustained no physical consequences himself (whereas the mother in *Goodwill* had become pregnant as a consequence of the negligence).

17 This will be of more difficulty in wrongful birth cases where causation is made out on the mother's evidence that had she known of the disability or risk of disability she would have undergone a termination: this key evidence may well be absent where it is the father alone bringing a claim.

- Whether the recoverability of damages would be different in claims brought in contract instead of in tort. Following the decision in *ARB v IVF Hammersmith and R* it appears that it makes no difference whether a claim is brought in contract or tort, and in either case no damages will be awarded for the maintenance costs of a healthy child. However, *ARB v IVF Hammersmith and R* has an appeal outstanding and so it remains to be seen whether the Court of Appeal will take the same view. One issue that was also left open was whether or not in a claim brought under contract the claimant would be entitled to a conventional award of £15,000.

- The interplay between legislation and the common law:

    - The *Congenital Disabilities (Civil Liability) Act 1976* appears to permit children who suffer from disabilities as a result of negligent pre-implantation genetic diagnosis to bring a claim: this would be akin to a wrongful life action as it would necessarily entail an argument that some other different embryo ought to have been selected. This result would be inconsistent with the common law.

    - The *Social Security (Recovery of Benefits) Act 1987* operates so that where a payment is made by a defendant in respect of an injury, illness or disease then the defendant is liable to reimburse the state for benefits received by the claimant. *Rand v East Dorset Health Authority (Deduction of Benefits)*[18] addressed whether the act applied to wrongful birth claims: it was held that it went too far to extend the act to cover a damages claim for pure economic loss (which is how the claim for the maintenance costs associated with the child's disability in *Rand* were categorised). As such in *Rand* deductions were made in accordance with the common law

18 [2001] P.I.W.R. Q1

instead,[19] and these did not include any deductions on account of the invalid care allowance the parents had received. *Rand* was decided prior to *Rees* and so it is unclear to what extent the damages now recoverable in wrongful birth and wrongful conception cases would be reduced pursuant to this act.

- Whether a claim for wrongful birth or wrongful conception falls within the scope of the *Damages Act 1996* so as to enable a periodical payment order (PPO) to be made by a court in respect of any damages claimed for the extra maintenance costs associated with a child's disability.[20] As above the approach of the Court of Appeal when addressing limitation issues was to categorise the whole of the damages claim, including maintenance costs, as a personal injury claim; if that approach was taken then there would be no reason why a PPO could not be made. This is not however an issue on which there has been a final determination.[21]

As a new wave of wrongful conception and wrongful birth cases come before the courts it may be that the Court of Appeal or even the Supreme Court provide answers to some of these remaining areas of uncertainty.

19 Specifically, per *Hodgson v Trapp* [1989] A.C. 807.

20 See discussion of this issue in two applications in *FP v Taunton and Somerset NHS Trust* [2009] EWHC 1965 at [6] and [2011] EWHC 3380 at [24].

21 It is of course open to the parties to an action to seek to agree to compromise the claim on the basis of periodical payments where this is possible as was suggested in *FP v Taunton and Somerset NHS Trust* [2009] EWHC 1965 at [6].

Time for a Re-Think?

Lessons Learned

Were a wrongful life, wrongful conception or wrongful birth claim to come before the courts in future then some important lessons can be learned from the progression of these types of cases through the courts so far. These include:

- ***Transparency:*** In *Emeh v Kensington and Chelsea Area Health Authority*[22] the Court of Appeal was heavily influenced by Peter Pain J in *Thake v Maurice.*[23]. This shows the benefit of transparency in reasoning: where the courts are explicit about policy considerations and the way in which these operate on decision making then this ensures that the appropriate balancing exercise can be undertaken to properly engage with the competing interests in a case. Subsequent satellite litigation can also be avoided where transparent reasoning is deployed.

- ***Acknowledging the difficulties openly and then responding to them:*** The difficulty in calculating damages in wrongful conception, wrongful birth and wrongful life claims has often been cited as one of the reasons against permitting recovery.

  The difficulty in balancing the mix of emotional and financial benefits and detriments which arise in wrongful conception and wrongful birth cases was initially addressed by Lord Cullen, delivering judgment in *McFarlane*, in the Inner House. He provided the example of a miner who had lost a limb at the fault of his employer, asserting that in that case no one would suggest that the benefits he now gained from having to work somewhere other than the mines, likely in an environment much less oppressive, should be deducted from the compensation that he would receive for the loss of a limb. This change in work, although properly construed as a benefit, was inexorably

22 [1985] Q.B. 1012; discussed in full in Chapter Four.

23 [1986] Q.B. 644; discussed in full in Chapter Four.

attached to an injury he would not have suffered but for the negligence of his employer.[24]

There is no reason why wrongful conception and wrongful birth claims should be any different. Although a child may bring benefits like those the miner enjoys, the very fact of that child's existence is a legal wrong that has been suffered by its parents, and one for which compensation can be provided (my emphasis).[25] The function of the courts is to respond to any difficulty in calculating damages, rather than simply denying recovery altogether.[26]

- ***Setting adequate parameters on recovery:*** It is not suggested that there ought to be no limitations on recovery. In fact, some limitation is probably necessary in order to meet policy concerns and to thereby prevent judicial, social, and parliamentary discord as well as to promote justice between the parties. Variable and unpredictable awards are also obviously undesirable. Were there to be a reasonable limit placed on an award for maintenance costs this would recognise the legal wrong and damage caused without making any statement as to the value of a child's life, without delving into the realms of impossible offset calculations, and without assigning liability for disproportionate damages to the clinician.

  The problem demonstrated consistently both in the cases which came before, and those which have come after, *McFarlane,* is that the courts are left to grapple with complex quantum issues with little guidance on how they should proceed. The difficulty in providing such guidance is that the list of those expenses which might be included in maintenance costs could not be

24 *McFarlane v Tayside Health Board* 1998 S.C. 389 (IH) at 403

25 *Ibid.*

26 See commentary in this regard in *Udale v Bloomsbury Area Health* Authority [1983] 1 WLR 1098 at 1107; *McFarlane v Tayside Health Board* [2000] 2 A.C. 59 at 103; *Allan v Greater Glasgow Health Board* 1998 S.L.T. 580.

foreseen in totality, and the task of listing everything that should or should not form part of an award is a cumbersome one. Were the Supreme Court to re-visit the recoverability of damages in these cases then a solution would need to be found, perhaps by setting a cap on damages or indicating a fixed sum for all cases (similar to the conventional award but properly reflecting the maintenance costs through a standard measure such as the actuarial cost of raising the 'average child,' for example).

- ***Avoiding emotive language / amending the terminology used:*** There is force in the argument made by Kirby J in his dissent in *Harriton v Stephens,*[27] that using the word 'wrongful' in these types of claims can be a bar to dispassionate logical analysis, which opens the door to emotive or moral reasoning and propounds value judgments. There is also a risk of confusion in the current terminology given the potential for the creation of new areas of negligence in line with medical advancements; the inadequacy of the current terminology caused the Supreme Court in Singapore to create a new type of wrong, that of wrongful fertilisation, in the case of *ACB v Thomson Medical Pte Ltd and Others.*[28] Were the issue to come back before the courts then it might be prudent to re-visit the way in which these types of claims are described in English law.

- ***Acceptance that pregnancy and childbirth is a real injury to women and that unwanted parenthood affects both the mother and the father:*** The fact that the Court of Appeal had to determine whether or not pregnancy and childbirth could be classed as personal injury[29] is indicative of a previous failure by the courts to address the real damage caused to a woman suffering this type of negligence. Viewing a child as a blessing in all cases is overly simplistic and does not recognise the legal wrong

---

27 [2006] HCA 15.

28 [2017] SGCA 20; discussed in full in Chapter Twelve.

29 See *Walkin v South Manchester Health Authority* [1995] 1 WLR 1543.

> implicit in the conception or birth of that child, nor the financial and practical implications of rearing that child. When individuals exercise a reproductive choice such as sterilisation, this provides absolute evidence that they did not judge the birth of a child and parenthood to be in their interests, nor a good thing for their own life. A greater focus on patient autonomy and gender equality should also be present in any future decisions in these areas.[30]

Is a Change Possible?

In *McFarlane*, *Parkinson* and *Rees* the reasoning was based on the following pillars:

1. What was fair, just and reasonable.
2. Distributive justice.
3. Legal policy.

In *McKay* the reasoning was largely based on the sanctity of life and the impossibility of comparing existence with non-existence for the purposes of calculating damages.

The tests which were used as the basis for rejecting either the claim in its entirety (for wrongful life) or the head of damages which included maintenance costs for a healthy child (wrongful conception and wrongful birth), are all capable of re-assessment with a change in social morality and policy considerations. Cast against a different framework of values, whether in society as whole or within the legal system, the outcome of these tests may well be different.

30 Which is beginning to be reflected in other areas of clinical negligence, as is discussed below.

The Sanctity of Life

The sanctity of life and the difficulty or impossibility of calculating damages have formed part of the reasoning in both wrongful life and wrongful conception / wrongful birth cases.

Since these key decisions in these areas there have however been times when the court have been asked to make determinations on whether it is in the best interests of a disabled or severely ill adult, or even child, to continue living or to be permitted to die. These end-of-life decisions recognise that sometimes dying is in fact the better outcome to living and so challenge traditional assumptions regarding the sanctity of life. As early as 1993 (though some 5 years after *McKay* had been decided) the House of Lords recognised that although the principle of the sanctity of life was important, it was not an absolute consideration.[31]

Of particular public interest have been legal decisions to withdraw life-saving treatment from children. These cases have captured media attention across the globe and have demonstrated that, often contrary to the parents' wishes and public opinion, the courts are willing to make decisions to allow children to die. Some high-profile cases include:

- Charlotte Wyatt, 2004 – 2006: Charlotte was born three months premature, suffering from severe organ damage, and was expected to die without medical assistance. Her own medical team requested an order from the court which permitted them to withhold artificial ventilation from her if her condition were to deteriorate, since she would have such a poor quality of life were she to continue to live. The Court of Appeal held that it was in the best interests of Charlotte that no artificial ventilation should be provided.[32]

---

31 *Airedale NHS Trust v Bland* [1993] A.C. 789.

32 For further information see *Portsmouth NHS Trust v Wyatt* [2004] EWHC 2457; *Portsmouth NHS Trust v Wyatt* [2005] EWHC 117 (Fam); *Portsmouth NHS Trust v Wyatt* [2005] EWCA 1181, [2005] 1 W.L.R. 3995; *Portsmouth NHS Trust v Wyatt* [2005] EWHC 693 (Fam).

- Baby OT, 2009: Baby OT was suffering from a genetic condition which caused him to become severely unwell. His medical team obtained orders and declarations allowing ventilation to be withdrawn.[33]

- Charlie Gard, 2017: Charlie was born with a congenital disease and his medical team applied to the court for permission to withdraw artificial ventilation, without which Charlie would die. This was contrary to his own parents' wishes, and they applied to the court to take him to the United States of America for experimental treatment, which was opposed by his medical team. The Court of Appeal eventually ruled that Charlie's life support ought to be switched off (and the European Court of Human Rights held that this decision did not violate Charlie's human rights, or those of his parents). Charlie's parents later withdrew their own application to take their son to America for experimental treatment.[34]

- Alfie Evans, 2018: Alfie was almost 2 years old when he fell in to a coma. His medical team applied for an order to withdraw ventilation, which was opposed by his parents. The order was nonetheless granted by Hayden J in the High Court, who held that withdrawing ventilation was in Alfie's best interests.[35] The Court of Appeal upheld that decision and permission to appeal was then denied by the Supreme Court. The European Court of Human Rights also rejected the case by Alfie's parents, finding there to be no human rights violation in issue and refusing to grant a stay on the High Court order. At the time of writing the

---

33 *OT, Re* [2009] EWHC 633 (Fam).

34 For further information see *Great Ormond Street Hospital for Children NHS Foundation Trust v Yates* [2017] EWHC 1909 (Fam), [2017] 4 W.L.R. 131; *Gard v United Kingdom (Admissibility) (39793/17)* [2017] 2 F.L.R. 773, (2017) 65 E.H.R.R. SE9; *Great Ormond Street Hospital for Children NHS Foundation Trust v Yates* [2017] EWCA Civ 410, [2018] 4 W.L.R. 5; *Great Ormond Street Hospital for Children NHS Foundation Trust v Yates* [2017] EWHC 972 (Fam).

35 [2018] EWHC 308 (Fam).

Court of Appeal is due to hear another appeal by Alfie's parents relating to the end-of-life care for their son.

In the cases above the courts are clearly demonstrating a willingness not only to compare non-existence with existence (something said to be an impossibility in the judgments of *McKay*) but also to find, on more than one occasion, that non-existence was the better outcome.[36]

What began with Charlotte Wyatt over a decade ago is still continuing today, as recently as within a month of the conclusion of writing: it is plainly not a case that a one-off or exceptional set of circumstances enabled the courts to reach a decision against the continued assisted life of these children. Although in a different factual context to wrongful life claims these decisions must be seen as sitting somewhat at odds with the reasoning employed in *McKay* against permitting a wrongful life claim. They also challenge much of the reasoning, that life will always be seen as a blessing, behind wrongful conception and wrongful birth claims. The law does however recognise a distinction between cases like the above, which concern the withdrawal of treatment, and cases which amount to euthanasia.[37] The sanctity of life does therefore remain a consideration for the courts, though it is clear from these recent cases that it now seems to be less of a bar to a claim that the principle of the sanctity of life might be offended by a certain outcome.

Autonomy and Gender Equality

There has also been a greater judicial acceptance of patient autonomy, as was evident in *Montgomery v Lanarkshire Health Board.*[38] In *Montgomery* the Supreme Court re-visited one of its own decisions and departed from it, in part relying on the change in social and legal approaches towards clinical treatment and patient autonomy.

---

36 This was also highlighted in Kirby J's dissent in *Harriton v Stephens* [2006] HCA 15 at [95].

37 See for example *Purdy v DPP* [2009] UKHL 45.

38 [2015] UKSC 11.

Patient autonomy is of central importance to wrongful conception and wrongful birth claims, where the consequences of negligence significantly affect the autonomy of the parents. Although the conventional award created in *Rees v Darlington Memorial Hospital NHS Trust*[39] was first suggested by Lord Millett in recognition of the affront to personal autonomy it is not clear whether the remainder of the majority in *Rees* would have created the conventional award for the same reasons. It is also arguable that the award is insufficient for those purposes, the amount falling far short of even the financial responsibility which is thrust upon the parent of a child born out of negligence.

It is clear from cases such as *Montgomery* that there has been a shift in the approach of the courts, with patient autonomy now being recognised as a paramount consideration. This may in turn lend support to the argument that the way damages are currently awarded in wrongful conception and wrongful birth cases does not adequately reflect that the negligence in these cases has infringed upon that important right.

Closely connected to the focus on autonomy in such cases is the need to ensure gender equality within society and the legal system. As Hale LJ first acknowledged in *Parkinson v St James and Seacroft University Hospital NHS Trust*[40] the issues surrounding wrongful conception and wrongful birth claims have a significant impact on women's rights. Lady Hale is now the President of the Supreme Court. Her judgment in *Parkinson* (when she sat as a member of the Court of Appeal) certainly does not present a glowing endorsement of *McFarlane* and emphasises the profound impact negligence in wrongful conception and wrongful birth cases has on women. With two female Supreme Court Judges, including Lady Hale as President, it is possible that the approach taken towards wrongful conception and wrongful birth claims would be different.

So too do considerations of gender equality come into play in cases concerning the father: as we have seen in *Whitehead v Searle*[41] it is not clear that the father in wrongful conception and wrongful birth claims would

39 [2004] 1 A.C. 309; discussed in full in Chapter Seven.

40 [2001] EWCA Civ 530; discussed in full in Chapter Six.

have a stand-alone cause of action. It would surely be an undesirable outcome were the courts to find that the father did not have a cause of action in his own right: the father is affected by the consequences of conception and birth in the same way as a mother, save for the intrusion in bodily integrity which the mother will also have to endure through pregnancy and childbirth.

Whitehead also demonstrated the potential unfairness which can arise because of the distinction the law currently draws between wrongful life and wrongful birth claims (cases which, as has been explored in other chapters, often concern the same facts but are brought by different claimants). In *Whitehead* a needy disabled child was left with no damages from which to benefit simply because the mother (who was able to bring a claim) had died and so her claim had died with her. This outcome was described in *Whitehead* as an intentional gap in the law, which had been established in *McKay*. As *Whitehead* was a claim brought in a professional negligence setting the court was not required to determine whether the father would have been able to bring a claim. The child in *Whitehead* was left with no damages claim whatsoever, simply by virtue of the 'bad luck' of having had a mother die and limitation expire before the father had any need to become involved in the claim. In *McKay* itself the child had the benefit of a mother, who was also bringing a wrongful birth claim, and of a continuing viable claim (in that case the child was still able to benefit from a damages award). Were a case with similar facts to *Whitehead* to come before the Supreme Court then it might be that the court would be more sympathetic to the plight of the child were the wrongful life claim rejected.

Medical Advancements

The legal system is required to continually evolve in order to meet the challenges presented by advancements in science and medicine. This has been evident with the introduction of legislation and new issues

---

41 [2008] EWCA Civ 285, [2009] 1 W.L.R. 549. also known as *McLeish (Deceased), Re Hibbert Pownall & Newton (A Firm) v Whitehead*; discussed in full in Chapter Nine

coming before the courts for determination in relation to new medical technologies and fertility treatments.

The court in *McKay* placed reliance on the *Congenital Disabilities (Civil Liability) Act 1976* ('the Congenital Disabilities Act') as providing support for the rejection of a wrongful life claim.[42] The view of the court in *McKay* was that the Congenital Disabilities Act was to be interpreted as rejecting any claim for wrongful life. However, in response to new available fertility treatment, the Congenital Disabilities Act was amended by the *Human Fertilisation and Embryology Act 1990.* This Act came in to force in 1990, after *McKay* had been decided, and introduced a new ground for liability under the Congenital Disabilities Act (for negligent pre-implantation diagnosis in IVF).[43] As has been discussed in previous chapters this new section potentially opens the door to a claim under the Congenital Disabilities Act on similar facts to what would otherwise be a (presently impermissible) wrongful life claim under common law. It is not clear what impact this addition would have had on the reasoning in *McKay*, but it is clear that with medical advancements come new issues for courts to consider which might impact the reasoning in previous wrongful life, wrongful conception and wrongful birth claims.

This was also made apparent in the recent case of *XX v Whittington NHS Trust.*[44] This was a claim involving a negligent failure to detect cervical cancer which resulted in the claimant's infertility. The court was assessing quantum of damages, and in particular whether the claimant was entitled to the costs of commercial surrogacy in California. It was held that she was not permitted to claim such damages since commercial surrogacy arrangements were illegal in the United Kingdom and so to award damages for the same would be contrary to public policy. The claimant argued that policy considerations had moved on since 2001, particularly given the introduction of new legis-

---

42 [1982] Q.B. 1166 at 1186 – 1187 and 1191 – 1192; discussed in full in Chapter Three.

43 See Section 1A(1)(b) of the *Congenital Disabilities (Civil Liability) Act 1976.*

44 [2017] EWHC 2318 (Q.B.); [2018] PIQR Q2.

lation under the *Human Fertilisation and Embryology Act 2008.* The claimant has been granted permission to appeal on the basis that determination of the issue is in the public interest (although there was no realistic prospect of success it was arguable that the law required clarification, taking in to account the legislation in force). Even though the claimant was unsuccessful her claim indicates how medical advancements and available fertility options can raise new issues for consideration, and the court in providing permission to appeal also acknowledged that.

Conclusions

The progression of wrongful life, wrongful conception and wrongful birth cases through the courts has historically demonstrated a reliance on policy to restrict the damages which are able to be claimed as a result of negligence which results in the birth of a child. More recently there have been challenges to the status quo, which reflect un-tested areas in these types of cases and present an opportunity for the Supreme Court to re-visit these controversial areas of law.

Policy considerations have clearly developed over time, whether in relation to medical advancements or in response to a changing landscape in respect of the legal and social views on sanctity of life and gender equality. However, not all policy considerations have developed in favour of allowing a wrongful life, wrongful conception or wrongful birth claim. One of the policy considerations which undoubtedly operated at the time that *McFarlane*, *Parkinson* and *Rees* were decided was in relation to a struggling NHS, against which any damages claim would be enforced, so taking much needed public funds away from the provision of medical services. That is not a consideration which has lessened in force over time: if anything, the NHS is more heavily burdened today. This concern must also be seen in light of continued government influence to reduce a perceived 'compensation culture' in society. Both of these are likely to be huge policy factors tending against expanding recovery of damages in wrongful life, wrongful conception and wrongful birth claims and will certainly influence any future decision of the Supreme Court.

Of course, were a wrongful conception, wrongful birth or wrongful life case to come before the Supreme Court then the Supreme Court would be re-visiting one of its own earlier decisions. Were the Supreme Court minded to make a different finding in relation to the recoverability of damages in wrongful conception and wrongful birth claims or the viability of wrongful life claims at all then their Lordships would need to satisfy themselves that there were sufficient grounds for departing from those earlier decisions.[45] We have seen a recent willingness to re-visit previous decisions in the Supreme Court: *Montgomery v Lanarkshire Health Board* is one such example in a clinical negligence setting.[46] Plainly where times have moved on since previous decisions and a change in the law is necessary to reflect current practices and modern attitudes, then the Supreme Court will be open to departing from a previous decision.[47]

With over 30 years having elapsed since the last decision on wrongful life and almost 15 years having elapsed since the last decision at Supreme Court level in wrongful conception and wrongful birth cases, it is perhaps time for the Supreme Court to re-visit wrongful life, wrongful conception and wrongful birth claims to ensure that the law properly reflects and responds to a changing legal and social climate, medical advancements and modern values.

---

45 A full discussion of the law surrounding the right of the Supreme Court to depart from an earlier Supreme Court decision is outside the scope of this book. For further information see the Practice Statement (Judicial Precedent) [1966]1 WLR 1234. Commentary in a wrongful conception / wrongful birth setting can also be found in *Rees v Darlington Memorial Hospital NHS Trust* [2004] 1 A.C. 309.

46 [2015] UKSC 11.

47 Recently evident in a personal injury setting as well, see *Knauer v Ministry of Justice* [2016] UKSC 9.

MORE BOOKS BY LAW BRIEF PUBLISHING

A selection of our other titles available now:

'A Practical Guide to Advising Schools on Employment Law' by Jonathan Holden
'Certificates of Lawful Use and Development: A Guide to Making and Determining Applications' by Bob Mc Geady & Meyric Lewis
'A Practical Guide to the Law of Dilapidations' by Mark Shelton
'A Practical Guide to the 2018 Jackson Personal Injury and Costs Reforms' by Andrew Mckie
'A Guide to Consent in Clinical Negligence Post-Montgomery' by Lauren Sutherland QC
'A Practical Guide to Running Housing Disrepair and Cavity Wall Claims: 2nd Edition' by Andrew Mckie & Ian Skeate
'A Practical Guide to the General Data Protection Regulation (GDPR)' by Keith Markham
'A Practical Guide to Digital and Social Media Law for Lawyers' by Sherree Westell
'A Practical Guide to Holiday Sickness Claims, 2nd Edition' by Andrew Mckie & Ian Skeate
'A Practical Guide to Inheritance Act Claims by Adult Children Post-Ilott v Blue Cross' by Sheila Hamilton Macdonald
'A Practical Guide to Elderly Law' by Justin Patten
'Arguments and Tactics for Personal Injury and Clinical Negligence Claims' by Dorian Williams
'A Practical Guide to QOCS and Fundamental Dishonesty' by James Bentley
'A Practical Guide to Drone Law' by Rufus Ballaster, Andrew Firman, Eleanor Clot
'Practical Mediation: A Guide for Mediators, Advocates, Advisers, Lawyers, and Students in Civil, Commercial, Business, Property, Workplace, and Employment Cases' by Jonathan Dingle with John Sephton
'Practical Horse Law: A Guide for Owners and Riders' by Brenda Gilligan

- ‘A Comparative Guide to Standard Form Construction and Engineering Contracts’ by Jon Close
- ‘A Practical Guide to Compliance for Personal Injury Firms Working With Claims Management Companies’ by Paul Bennett
- ‘A Practical Guide to the Landlord and Tenant Act 1954: Commercial Tenancies’ by Richard Hayes & David Sawtell
- ‘A Practical Guide to Personal Injury Claims Involving Animals’ by Jonathan Hand
- ‘A Practical Guide to Psychiatric Claims in Personal Injury’ by Liam Ryan
- ‘Introduction to the Law of Community Care in England and Wales’ by Alan Robinson
- ‘A Practical Guide to Dog Law for Owners and Others’ by Andrea Pitt
- ‘Ellis and Kevan on Credit Hire, 5th Edition’ by Aidan Ellis & Tim Kevan
- ‘RTA Allegations of Fraud in a Post-Jackson Era: The Handbook, 2nd Edition’ by Andrew Mckie
- ‘RTA Personal Injury Claims: A Practical Guide Post-Jackson’ by Andrew Mckie
- ‘On Experts: CPR35 for Lawyers and Experts’ by David Boyle
- ‘An Introduction to Personal Injury Law’ by David Boyle
- ‘A Practical Guide to Claims Arising From Accidents Abroad and Travel Claims’ by Andrew Mckie & Ian Skeate
- ‘A Practical Guide to Cosmetic Surgery Claims’ by Dr Victoria Handley
- ‘A Practical Guide to Chronic Pain Claims’ by Pankaj Madan
- ‘A Practical Guide to Claims Arising from Fatal Accidents’ by James Patience
- ‘A Practical Approach to Clinical Negligence Post-Jackson’ by Geoffrey Simpson-Scott
- ‘A Practical Guide to Personal Injury Trusts’ by Alan Robinson
- ‘Occupiers, Highways and Defective Premises Claims: A Practical Guide Post-Jackson’ by Andrew Mckie
- ‘Employers' Liability Claims: A Practical Guide Post-Jackson’ by Andrew Mckie

'A Practical Guide to Subtle Brain Injury Claims' by Pankaj Madan
'The Law of Driverless Cars: An Introduction' by Alex Glassbrook
'A Practical Guide to Costs in Personal Injury Cases' by Matthew Hoe
'A Practical Guide to Alternative Dispute Resolution in Personal Injury Claims – Getting the Most Out of ADR Post-Jackson' by Peter Causton, Nichola Evans, James Arrowsmith
'A Practical Guide to Personal Injuries in Sport' by Adam Walker & Patricia Leonard
'A Practical Guide to Marketing for Lawyers' by Catherine Bailey & Jennet Ingram
'The No Nonsense Solicitors' Practice: A Guide To Running Your Firm' by Bettina Brueggemann
'Baby Steps: A Guide to Maternity Leave and Maternity Pay' by Leah Waller
'The Queen's Counsel Lawyer's Omnibus: 20 Years of Cartoons from the Times 1993-2013' by Alex Steuart Williams

These books and more are available to order online direct from the publisher at www.lawbriefpublishing.com, where you can also read free sample chapters. For any queries, contact us on 0844 587 2383 or mail@lawbriefpublishing.com.

Our books are also usually in stock at www.amazon.co.uk with free next day delivery for Prime members, and at good legal bookshops such as Hammicks and Wildy & Sons.

We are regularly launching new books in our series of practical day-to-day practitioners' guides. Visit our website and join our free newsletter to be kept informed and to receive special offers, free chapters, etc.

You can also follow us on Twitter at www.twitter.com/lawbriefpub.

www.ingramcontent.com/pod-product-compliance
Lightning Source LLC
LaVergne TN
LVHW052327200926
848481LV00002B/692

9781911035565